JESUS ONE OF US

Bible Studies on the Person of Jesus Christ

Edited by
Brede Kristensen
& Ada Lum

InterVarsity Press
Downers Grove
Illinois 60515

© 1976 by the International Fellowship of Evangelical Students. Printed in America by InterVarsity Press, Downers Grove, Illinois, with permission from the International Fellowship of Evangelical Students, 10 College Road, Harrow, Middlesex, HA1 1BE, England.

InterVarsity Press is the book-publishing division of Inter-Varsity Christian Fellowship, a student movement active on campus at hundreds of universities, colleges and schools of nursing. For information about local and regional activities, write IVCF, 233 Langdon St., Madison, WI 53703.

Distributed in Canada through InterVarsity Press, 1875 Leslie St., Unit 10, Don Mills, Ontario M3B 2M5, Canada.

The Bible quotations in this book, unless otherwise indicated, are from the Revised Standard Version of the Bible, copyrighted in 1946 and 1971 by the Division of Christian Education, National Council of Churches of Christ in the USA.

ISBN 0-87784-618-9

Printed in the United States of America

17	16	15	14	13	12	11	10	9	8	7	6	5	4	3	2	1
95	94	93	92	91	90	89	88	87	86	85	84	83	82	81		

Contents

Foreword

I remember climbing out of a swimming pool in Singapore when an English naval officer approached me and blurted out, "Thank God for Ada Lum!" I was naturally surprised at this unusual compliment. Seeing my puzzled countenance, this officer went on to explain that he became a committed Christian after working through Ada Lum's evangelistic Bible study guide, *Jesus the Radical*.

This man met Jesus Christ as he studied the records of his life with others aboard their naval frigate. Countless numbers of students have been led to investigate in greater depth the person, character, teaching and work of Christ through such open Bible discussions.

This spirit of open discussion is important today. Most students are wary of political, commercial and religious propaganda. Asian students do not like to be button-holed by Christians who simply spout Bible texts or some evangelistic formula at them.

But if they can unhurriedly in an informal setting examine the accounts of Jesus' life and teaching, they are often led to a face-to-face encounter with the living person of Jesus Christ. Then they can no longer regard him as a great religious teacher worshipped only by the "whites". They begin to see him indeed as the man of men — the man for others. Like two of Jesus' disciples, they are led further to acknowledge him as "the Christ, the Son of the living God" and as "my Lord and my God!"

It is sad that university students in Europe, North America and Africa still cherish classroom or Sunday school notions of Jesus Christ. As such, they find him utterly irrelevant to their needs and to the pressing problems of modern society. Evangelistic Bible studies conducted by adults and for adults often open up new vistas to the uniqueness and relevance of the life and work of Jesus Christ.

The primary aim of the studies in *Jesus: One of Us* is to help participants (regardless of their religious affiliation or ecclesiastical pedigree) to a fresh understanding of Jesus Christ. Most of these studies have been tested and extensively used in different situations. The responses have varied from wholehearted commitment to Christ to a temporary rejection of his claims on the lives of the participants who have found his presence and standards too disturbing and shattering. In both responses, the decisions are based on a careful study and evaluation of the evidence and data, not on second-hand knowledge or subjective opinion. It is the prayer of the writers and editors that those who use this compilation will meet the living Lord Jesus in a new and vigorous way.

Jesus: One of Us is in reality a collective effort. These studies have been written, revised, edited and typed by a team of gifted and dedicated workers from six continents. It is impossible to trace and acknowledge every contributor individually. The major credits go to the untiring labours of two of our field staff and colleagues — Ada Lum and Brede Kristensen. They have been ably supported by their two patient and persevering secretaries, Miss Lim Tar Kian (Singapore) and Miss Pauline Beacham (London). We gratefully acknowledge the assistance of the FES, Singapore staff, who joined hands with the IFES team in the final stages of the production of this book.

May *Jesus: One of Us* be used to the spiritual enrichment of many!

London
July, 1976

Chua Wee Hian
General Secretary, IFES

Introduction

You must be something like us, if you're interested enough to pick up this book. You want to know who Jesus Christ is and discover his relevance for modern life, and perhaps for your own life, by turning to the four accounts of his life recorded in the Bible. We hope that this book will answer some of your questions and will mean something in your life.

Or perhaps you are like some of us, rather inexperienced Bible study leaders. Or some of us who want to train others to lead new study groups. So you want practical help in evangelistic Bible study guides. We also have wanted such guides. We need the kind which don't assume that we know much about the Bible or that our friends know how to study it.

We need the kind that have built-in help for the leader, i.e., background information, textual notes and even titled subdivisions to help us see and remember the structure of the passage. And we need the kind that have questions which make us search the text itself — which lead us to think hard about its meaning — and which challenge us to realistic applications.

We are thirty students and staff from nearly as many countries. We wrote these study guides in various writing workshops during international student conferences and national staff sessions. We helped each other by evaluating and suggesting improvements. Then we asked some relatively experienced people to edit the results. We field-tested them in our countries and made further changes.

It's been rather exciting to see God already use them to bring people to himself. And we ourselves have been mentally and spiritually exhilarated by the very experience of digging deeper into the Bible and discovering new insights into God's purposes and way of thinking. Though some of us have been Christians for some time, we've seen Jesus Christ in more new, life-changing ways.

We pray these joys for you, too, as you begin to use them.

London/Singapore
July, 1976

Brede Kristensen/Ada Lum
for the Thirty Writers

Help for Leaders

Studying with Seeking Friends

Many sincere seekers interested in your faith in Jesus Christ will not join you in a church meeting. They are apt to feel overwhelmed by the Christian majority. They are more likely to join you in a small group study in a home, or office, or classroom or public garden. Still others will be comfortable discussing personal religious matters only privately with you.

An alert Christian can be like Philip having a one-to-one evangelistic Bible study (EBS) with an overseas seeker in a royal limousine (Acts 8:26-40). Or she can be like Priscilla with an Aquila "explaining the way of God more accurately" to a sincere but inadequately instructed believer like Apollos after the public meeting (Acts 18:26). But don't stop here. Be ambitious for Jesus Christ and his kingdom. Perhaps he wants you to be a Lydia or a Philemon, whose homes turned into evangelistic and discipling communities where people became believers (Acts 16:15, 40 and Philemon 2).

Next to prayerful dependence upon God's Spirit for your personal preparation and the group study, understanding your seeking friends is most important. Otherwise you cannot know their real needs. For instance, a non-Christian's ignorance of the Bible does not mean he is not able to think through a Bible text. Because the Bible is fresh to him, he often has insights that escape the Christian who is overfamiliar with the gospel stories, and perhaps with Jesus Christ himself!

Christians should always be ready to lead their seeking friends in the group to confront the Lord Jesus Christ personally. Most of these studies have a second or third question at the end to help bring the serious seeker to this point. "A Final Word" at the end of each series can also help to conclude significantly.

Must You Use All 52 Studies?

The eight series, though independent of each other, are complementary. Thus, if you read the introduction to each series and take even a cursory look at the titles, you can know what aspects of Christ's person and his work of salvation each emphasises, and therefore, which series is suitable for your group.

The two main parts of this compilation are divided like this: Part I, "Honest Answers to Honest Questions", concentrates on the seeker, his honest doubts in today's world, his aspirations for a wholesome life and his struggles to believe. Part II, "Who Then is Jesus Christ?" concentrates on the person of Jesus Christ — who he is, how he lived, what he taught, and what his life mission was. The last series is a clear-cut call to radical discipleship on Jesus' terms.

The Leader's Use of the Guide

As a wise leader you should regard the guide as a servant, not a master. First, make the study your own, hearing God speak to you and your situation. Then prepare with the group in mind.

The different parts of the guide are designed to help you prepare as adequately as possible, especially when you may be lacking Bible study aids like Bible dictionaries and commentaries. For instance, textual notes and cross references are more for your thorough understanding than for the members who may not raise those points at all. Likewise, subtitles should not be mechanically announced to the group, but they help you to remember the outline of the text, and so enable you to progress more smoothly from one main point to the next.

However, you should always include the brief context so that members can appreciate the continuity of Jesus' life and the historical nature of the gospel events. Otherwise they may sound like just another old legend or fairy tale.

The questions should never be used mechanically, but flexibly. They are intended to stimulate thoughtful, personal investigation of the Bible. You will find basically three types:

2

1) *observation questions* which cause the members to search the text irself, 2) *interpretation questions* which lead them to think together about its meaning, and 3) *application questions* which challenge them to realistic practice of the truth. (This last type is sometimes referred to as "practical themes", "implications", "reflections", etc.) Note that there is always a choice among two or three possible application themes. You can make the choice according to the interest or response of the members.

You should feel free to adapt the questions to the group's level and needs. Reword them to suit your personality. You may even omit some and add others. But you should always be careful not to lose the progression of ideas.

Leaders and Co-leaders

Though you are the designated leader, you should begin to look for co-leaders. They can be extremely helpful to you in being sensitive to what may be missing either in the study itself or in the members' personal interaction. You can eventually rotate with them in the designated leadership. Thus more leaders are trained to start new groups.

Good Bible study leaders are not lecturers or preachers. They are more like shepherds who guide their flocks to green pastures to feed for themselves. They do not push from behind, but rather move just a few steps ahead to show the way. They keep in mind that it is as important to promote fellowship as to cover the text in a study/discussion.

One of your basic responsibilities as leader is to watch that the discussion is based on the text. If it is based on subjective opinion or personal experience only, you could refer members back to the Bible by asking, "Where did you find that in our passage?" Or, "How did you arrive at that conclusion?" Or perhaps more pointedly, "I think I understand what you're saying. But how do you relate that to what Jesus is saying in v. 11?"

Throughout the study seek to maintain an atmosphere of love and openness, expectancy to learn from God, and humility to learn from each other. At the end it is good to give a short, clear conclusion, summarising the message of the

3

passage and its relevance to the group.

Group Members' Active Participation

Some groups, to whom Bible study is new, find it helpful to go through the questions one by one. These have been so prepared that inexperienced members can learn to observe what the text really says before drawing conclusions about its meaning.

Other groups are more experienced in inductive study; i.e., most members are used to carefully observing the text before interpreting its meaning. In such cases the leader can sometimes omit the more detailed textual (observation or factual) questions and move on to the interpretation questions.

In any case the wise leader encourages participation from all members, though he will not embarrass any shy ones. The more each member searches and thinks about the biblical text, the more interested he becomes, and the more responsible he will feel for the truth about Jesus Christ. As in any study/discussion, group members participate when they *listen, think and link.* They link to each other and to each other's ideas by —
 — expanding someone else's idea;
 — illustrating an important subject;
 — asking relevant questions, e.g., for clarification, for deeper examination of a significant point, or for more information;
 — tactfully correcting or modifying a point;
 — sharing themselves sincerely;
 — introducing a fresh viewpoint;
 — contributing in any way to help move the study along.

They may help someone reword a difficult or awkward question. They also can develop sensitivity to others and help relieve tensions that may arise in the group.

Prayer Throughout

Do not presume upon God's help, even though it is true that he is more eager than we that we understand his Word. Prayer opens up our lives to him personally and directly.

4

Prayer keeps our relationship healthily dependent on him. Prayer for our friends helps to bring divine wisdom in how to relate and communicate Jesus Christ to them.

When you prepare, pray for yourself, for the group members, for the study itself. In some EBS groups you may find it inappropriate to pray publicly, since some non-Christians may be embarrassed or feel excluded. (Other non-Christians may expect it!) But that doesn't mean God is less present, especially if you are silently trusting him.

And you'll surely want to continue praying afterwards when you can evaluate the study for improvements and understand better the response of your friends to Jesus Christ and his Word.

Abbreviations

Books of the Bible
Gn., Genesis; Ex., Exodus; Lv., Leviticus; Nu., Numbers; Dt., Deuteronomy; Ps., Psalm; Is., Isaiah; Dn., Daniel; Ho., Hosea.

Mt., Matthew; Mk., Mark; Lk., Luke; Jn., John; Ro., Romans.

General Abbreviations
c.	century
cf.	compare
ch.	chapter
E	east
e.g.	for example
Gk.	Greek
Heb.	Hebrew
i.e.	that is
lit.	literally
N	north
NT	New Testament
OT	Old Testament
S	south
v. vv.	verse, verses
W	west

Part I

Honest Answers
to Honest Questions

The first part of this book looks at Jesus Christ as seekers did when he was here on earth. Jesus Christ was a great question provoker. Everywhere he went people asked him questions. They also asked each other questions about this newcomer, his new life-style and "new teaching". Some asked questions dishonestly, for they did not want to be disturbed by this great Disturber.

But others asked questions honestly, for they wanted to know his answers. They instinctively knew that here was a man who knew what he was talking about when he answered them about life's basic, often agonising problems. Here they saw one who identified with others, who indeed was one of them. They saw their own humanity reflected in his life — the truth about themselves, not pretense.

When we today also question and ponder Jesus' answers to our authentic questions, we will begin to understand why he is called "a man of sorrows". For he has taken on our sorrows and sins, suffering what we suffer, feeling with us in our struggles to believe and aspire to reality and integrity.

But Jesus is also called "the Son of man", the bringer of life, for he has opened up the way out of our human sickness into God's health. The "good news" of which the Bible speaks is nothing more and nothing less than the news that Jesus Christ has come for us.

A Faith for Today

Your interest in this brief series of studies about some basic issues in life shows that you have an open, questioning mind that is willing to break out of your old routine. This attitude is precisely what is lacking today.

The truth about God and the Christian life comes to us through revelation. We know the physical world through simple observation, but we know other persons only if they reveal themselves and allow themselves to be known. God has revealed himself in Jesus Christ and the Bible so that we may know him.

Our study will center upon certain basic questions which are simple, but also profound and of transcendental importance. These questions deal with God, the human condition, freedom, the new man, and faith in Jesus Christ. Many of these words have been used so much today that they have virtually lost their meaning. Nevertheless, they do point to realities and problems which continue to challenge us in our day to day living.

We will be asking what the Bible has to say to these questions. The message of the One who speaks through the Bible has transformed the lives of millions of people from every race, era, social status and culture.

The following pages require your careful attention. It is worthwhile to give it! Jesus himself affirmed, "Seek and you will find."

(This series of evangelistic Bible studies was originally developed by the IFES in Latin America for a Bible correspondence course but used also in groups).

1 God and Man
Psalm 139:1-18, 23-24

The problem of many people today is that they have not found a God who is adequate to face the modern world. The God of the catechism or of our Sunday school children's stories is too small when one grows up and faces the heavy weight of life's complexities and problems.

What is God like? A fiery force that set the universe in motion millions of years ago? An impersonal mind? A kind of great cosmic policeman ready to rain down blows on whoever disagrees with him? A cold, distant Olympian personality who has little interest in the world?

So many strange concepts of God are abroad that if anyone declares himself an atheist, we must ask him which God he is denying. The atheist may well find himself in agreement with the Bible in refusing to believe in certain kinds of gods.

On the night of his conversion to Jesus Christ, the brilliant mathematician and philosopher, Blaise Pascal, wrote about the great discovery he had just made: "FIRE. . .the God of Abraham, the God of Isaac, the God of Jacob, not the God of the philosophers and the wise. . .certainty, joy, peace. The God of Jesus Christ." The God who reveals himself in Scripture had spoken to him.

We are going to examine a biblical passage in search of an answer to our question, what is God like?

Notes on the Text

v. 1ff   *Lord (Jahweh)* See Word List.
v. 2   *from afar* Long before.
v. 5   *beset* Encircle, surround.
v. 8   *Sheol* Dwelling place of the dead, good or evil; cf. Hades, hell.

v. 9   *wings of the morning* Cf. the speed of morning light.
v. 13   *inward parts* Lit. "kidneys", symbolising the seat of
        emotion and affection, the psychological aspects of
        man.

Comments and Questions for the Study

This passage is a psalm, written in poetic form. It is a
prayer — the words which one person directs to another person. Like the Bible as a whole, it characteristically expresses
profound truth in terms of personal experience.

For your study, follow these steps:
1. Read the whole psalm attentively. Re-read vv. 1-6
    carefully and try to capture the main idea expressed in
    them.
    What do you think this main idea is?
    Who is mentioned in these verses? (To answer this
    question, put yourself in the place of the author of
    the psalm. This was written with the idea that the
    reader would participate in the author's experience)
2. In vv. 1-5, what relation is there between the persons
    mentioned?
    Who takes the initiative in this relationship?
    Describe the nature of the relationship.
3. What does God know about me? (See vv. 2-4)
    To what different areas of my life do these verses
    refer?
    What are your reactions to the fact that God knows
    you this way?
4. Read v. 5. What would you know about God if you had
    only this verse?
    Have you ever felt the "hand of God" touching your
    life in any way?
    How did you respond to that experience?
5. How did the author respond to God? (Notice first v. 6,
    and then vv. 13-18. V. 14 summarises his reaction)
    What contrast does v. 7 express?
    What impossibility is expressed in vv. 7-12?
    Note vv. 23, 24. What other attitude do they express?
6. Summarise what this psalm has taught you about God.

For Personal Reflection

How can we get to the point where we are not bothered by God's knowing all that we are and do? How can we achieve a joyful relationship with him? Are you trying to run away from God?

Some people try to lose themselves in a never-ending rat race of activity, work and diversions. They fear that silence in which God might speak to them. Others want to reduce God to an idea and by this simple reasoning rid themselves of him. Both are forms of running away from God. What is needed is a way to return to God — to find peace with him.

"Therefore, since we are justified by faith, we have peace with God through our Lord Jesus Christ. Through him we have obtained access to this grace in which we stand." *Romans 5:1, 2*

What affirmations in Psalm 139 show us that this psalm mainly speaks about a man's personal relationship with God?

Describe in your own words what this psalm says God knows about any human personality.

The following studies will shed more light on this subject.

2 The Human Condition
Romans 1:18-32

Sin. A word which may provoke sarcastic smiles, or suggest scandalous images. A basic ingredient in a certain kind of romantic music. A brand of seductive perfume. Something to spice up the titles of some popular films. Is there anything more to it?

The key figures shaping modern thought have coined other phrases: the "alienation" of which Marx spoke; Freud's "neurotic dimension"; the "anguish" of the existentialists and Marcuse's "one-dimensional man". All these shed light on some aspect of our human condition with its strange mixture of misery and greatness. They give brief glimpses of different facets of that totality which the Bible calls sin, man's state of alienation from God.

Let us study this subject with the apostle Paul in his letter to the Romans, where he gives a devastating analysis of man and his destiny. We will only be examining a brief passage from this book which has had such a profound impact on the lives of St. Augustine, Martin Luther, John Wesley, and other important historical figures.

Notes on the Text

v. 18 *wrath of God* God's judgement because of his displeasure at men's moral evil.

   ungodliness The utter wrongness of pagan religion; cf. vv. 21-25.

   wickedness The utter wrongness of pagan morality; cf. vv. 26-32.

   the truth Cf. vv. 19-20, 25.

vv. 24, 26, 28 *God gave them up* Not a passive but an active punishment for such wilful ignorance and rebellion against their Creator.

Comments and Questions for the Study

Does your reading of this passage surprise you? Although it was written in the first century, it sounds very much like the front page of any newspaper today. As you take a closer look at the text, these steps will help you:

1. First, make a list of attitudes and actions which you would label "sin". If you don't have definite ideas on the subject yourself, then note down what others whose opinions you respect have considered "sin".

2. Now read vv. 18-23. Note the human actions mentioned here as examples of the "ungodliness and wickedness of men" (vv. 18, 21, 22, 23). How would human beings act if they did the opposite of what Paul describes?

    For example, instead of "suppressing the truth" (v. 18), they would be "proclaiming the truth".

    As you continue to make these contrasts, note that these human possibilities constitute a whole new reality.

3. Now list the human actions and attitudes described as sin in vv. 24-32.

    Compare this list with the list you made above. What are the differences?

    How does this broaden your understanding of what "sin" is?

4. What is the result of the situation described in the verses you have just studied? Note the expression "God gave them up" (vv. 24, 26, 28).

    Why did God do this? What do the phrases "therefore" (v. 24) and "for this reason" (v. 26) link to?

    What further explanation is given in v. 28?

5. Idolatry (vv. 23, 25) is the heart of the matter.

    Look carefully at v. 21.

    List the five facts, in their logical sequence, given here about mankind.

    In the situation in which we live today, what forms does our idolatry take?

6. How is the phrase, "although they knew God" (v. 21) related to v. 20?

    What specifically does the creation reveal about God?

7. Compare the phrase "they did not honour him as God" with v. 28. Explain the meaning in your own words.
   How do most men act today in relation to God?
   What different attitudes toward God have you encountered? Hostility? Ignorance? Apparent acceptance?

8. "They did not. . .give thanks to God" (v. 21). Think of the implications of giving thanks.
   What does it demonstrate in our relationships with other people?
   What consequences does it have?
   Now apply this to the relation between God and man.

9. "But they became futile in their thinking. . . ." (v. 21).
   Relate the whole content of v. 21 with v. 25, and note its centrality in this passage.
   How would you re-state this theme in your own words?

10. What is the origin of man's condemnable actions?
    Has your concept of "sin" changed?
    Summarise your conclusions by formulating your own definition of sin.

For Personal Reflection

Notice God's attitude toward sin in v. 18. What relation do you see between this and the desire to escape from God which we saw in Psalm 139?

Much has been said about the many forms which idolatry has taken in our times. We see it in modern ideologies and must face the ethical problems posed by idolising money, success, power, political parties, the state, race, etc. What is your idol? Do you believe that you have sinned against God? Have you thanked him by accepting yourself for what you are and have? Have you honoured him by giving him the place he deserves?

"For the wages of sin is death, but the free gift of God is eternal life in Christ Jesus our Lord." *Romans 6:23*

Continue your study to know more of the answer God offers to man's problems.

3 Slavery & Freedom
John 8:31-47

All of us want to be free, but how many of us achieve our goal? Much has been written on this subject, and since the twentieth century has seen so many different forms of oppression, several ideas have become clear.

As many have realised, the essence of freedom is to be free *from* something and to be free *for* something. What do we need to be freed from? Man is bound by any number of chains, but Jesus affirms that there is one basic slavery that affects all mankind. And he also says that he can liberate us from it.

In this study, we will enter into dialogue with Jesus through the pages of the New Testament. We will see him as an exceptional teacher, and a captivating and paradoxical personality. In the passage under our consideration, Jesus begins with a local problem tied to his society and his era, but he goes on to make affirmations of universal importance. As you read and think about the passage, try to put yourself into what was happening that day so that you can have your own dialogue with the Teacher.

Notes on the Text

v. 31   *believed*   "Committed oneself to", though superficially here.
disciples   Personal students/followers of a recognised teacher.

v. 33   *Abraham*   See Word List.

v. 41   *born of fornication*   An OT comparison to spiritual apostasy; cf. Hosea.

16

Comments and Questions for the Study

Our text narrates part of an encounter Jesus had with some of Jerusalem's religious leaders (his fellow Jews). Jesus' affirmation that the Jews want to kill him was no exaggeration. In fact, his frankness in the discussion with them raised the tension to such a high level that at the end of this chapter, the author tells us that they were enraged enough to pick up stones, intending to kill him.

1. Read this passage carefully, paying special attention to vv. 31-36. Who was Jesus addressing in v. 34? Your reading will show you that the group "who had believed in him" (v. 31) had only an initial enthusiasm which not only did not last, but actually turned into hostile aggression.

    Notice the harsh words of the Teacher in vv. 37, 44.

    Vv. 31, 32 mention three steps which must preceed freedom. What are they?

    If we are to be free, who should rule our lives (vv. 33-36)?

    What enslaves us?

    What relation can you see between truth and liberty?

2. For Jews like those talking with Jesus, their greatest pride was to be one of the "descendents of Abraham". This made them feel superior to their Roman conquerors. For this reason they were shocked by Jesus' statement in v. 33.

    They were thinking of political freedom, but according to v. 34, what more basic liberty did Jesus have in mind?

    Express his meaning in your own words.

3. Evaluate the condition of these Jews in the light of our previous study on the human condition, and the definition of sin which we arrived at.

    In what other specific ways does Jesus sharpen our understanding of the Jews' condition (vv. 42, 43, 47)?

    Why did these people not realise that they were enslaved?

What basic truth should they have opened their eyes to in the first place?

4. What does all of this mean to us today? Read v. 34 once again.

Note Jesus' universal affirmation regarding "every one".

Are you included in this?

As we have observed, sin is rejecting God, not giving thanks to him or recognising him for who he really is. The man who sins is a slave to sin. This slavery takes many forms —

— not finding a lasting source of satisfaction; running desperately after pleasure and falling prisoner to various vices;

— having high ideals but being unable to achieve them;

— living under a lie, with a false purpose in life.

What are other forms of slavery today?

5. Read vv. 31, 32 and 36 once again.

How are we liberated?

From what and for what are we liberated?

Write down the characteristics of the free person whom Jesus describes here.

For Personal Reflection

Many people are well aware of their enslavement. Think of the many things which enslave men today: habits, passions, material goods, institutions, ideologies.

What enslaves you? From what would you like to be free?

At this point in your life, are you free of man's basic slavery and its consequences? Who or what rules your life?

When a person recognises Jesus as Lord of his life, he is freed from his slavery to sin. God comes to occupy his rightful place in that person's life. The fruits of liberation begin to be seen. The risks and uncertainties of life are no longer a crushing load. The liberated person begins to discover what he is living for, to find lasting satisfaction, to break out of the vicious circle of selfishness and fear.

4 The New Man
John 3:1-16

If only I could begin all over again! How many times have we expressed this wish to ourselves? Other times we realise that we need a radical change in our lives. Many resolve to carry out those changes when the new year begins or when they have another birthday. But nothing changes. . . .

The "new man" is a favourite expression of the revolutionaries. For some it means the denial of everything bourgeois. For others it will be the person whose life and happiness are determined by science with mathematical precision. Where do we find these new men?

One time when Jesus was conversing with a Jewish intellectual, he used the expression to be "born anew". This conversation teaches us our need for a complete renovation of our being. We must obtain access to a completely different order of things, which, although difficult to understand, is within the grasp of every person. This is the beginning of a new quality of life which Jesus calls eternal life.

Notes on the Text

v. 1   *Pharisees* See Word List.
        ruler of the Jews: Member of the highest Jewish council. See Word List.
v. 2   *Rabbi* See Word List.
        signs Miracles. See John 2:23.
v. 10   *a teacher* "The teacher" (Gk), i.e. distinguished in Israel.
v. 16   *eternal!* See Word List.

Comments and Questions for the Study

This dialogue between Jesus and Nicodemus begins with a reference to the kingdom of God. In the Bible, this term refers to the sovereignty of God and his activity in governing the world. In other words, it refers to that transformed order of things in which our deepest desires become reality.

1. As you read the text, try to follow the thread of the dialogue. Nicodemus was an important man. Note what vv. 1 and 10 tell about the position which he occupied among his people.

    What attitude do his words in v. 2 reveal?

    What might be his reasons for visiting Jesus at night?

2. Like other Jews of his time, Nicodemus was awaiting the kingdom of God which the Messiah would inaugurate.

    To what unvoiced concern of Nicodemus might Jesus be responding in v. 3?

    Note the authoritative tone of Jesus' words, "Truly, truly, I say to you".

    What gave Jesus the authority to speak this way (vv. 2, 11, 13)?

3. For a man like Nicodemus, the only requirement for entering the kingdom of God was to be physically born a Jew.

    Taking this into account, what does his question in v. 4 express?

    To help Nicodemus understand his radical teaching, Jesus used contrasts — between two kingdoms, two births, and two different planes of reality.

    What is each one like? Compare vv. 5, 6, and 12.

    Notice especially the contrast between natural birth and spiritual rebirth. Who acts in this second birth? What characterises his activity? What is man's part in the rebirth?

4. What major point did Jesus illustrate in talking about the wind in v. 8?

    Notice what he stated about cause and effect.

Nicodemus' next question indicates he was still troubled by a related problem. What was that problem?
Some very simple things are difficult, even for teachers. The new birth is one of them.
What one simple thing did Jesus want Nicodemus to do (vv. 11, 12)?
Are you willing to accept Jesus and believe his words? Vv. 13-16 give several reasons for taking that step.

5. How could Jesus, the Son of Man, demand the faith and confidence of Nicodemus or of any other person? Think about this as you make a list of everything which vv. 13-16 tell us about Jesus.

V. 14 refers to an incident from Israel's history which took place when the nation was wandering in the wilderness. A plague of poisonous snakes had descended upon the people because of their rebellion. God provided the cure if they would only look at a bronze serpent which Moses had set upon a pole as the symbol. (If you have a Bible, you can read about the incident in the Old Testament book of Nu. 21:4-9)

Jesus' explanation and reference to himself through this illustration speaks about the totality of his work: God becomes man, dies on a cross and is raised again. Thus Jesus' death on the cross brings about the reconciliation between man and God.

6. As we have seen in our previous studies, man's problem today (as in Jesus' day) is sin — rejecting God, ignoring him, falling into idolatry. Both Nicodemus' situation and our own are like that of the rebellious Israelites.

What must we do if we are not to be lost (vv. 15, 16)?

For Personal Reflection

V. 16 is an excellent synthesis of the Gospel. What does it say regarding God? Regarding Jesus? Regarding you? Do you want to have the Spirit act in your life? Do you want to be born anew?

The apostle Paul explains the meaning of Jesus' cross in these words:

"For in him (Christ) all the fullness of God was pleased to dwell, and through him to reconcile to himself all things, whether on earth or in heaven, making peace by the blood of his cross. And you, who once were estranged and hostile in mind, doing evil deeds, he has now reconciled in his body of flesh by his death, in order to present you holy and blameless and irreproachable before him." *Colossians 1:19-22*

"Therefore, if any one is in Christ, he is a new creation, the old has passed away, behold, the new has come . . . . For our sake he (God) made him to be sin who knew no sin, so that in him we might become the righteousness of God." *2 Corinthians 5:17, 21*

Some people think that faith consists in *believing* that false things are true. The more improbable the thing to be believed, the greater the "faith" one must exercise. Others reduce faith to mere intellectual assent. They believe in God because they see the necessity of having a "first principle" for everything. This belief, however, has nothing to do with their daily life. Is this really what faith is?

In the Bible faith, or believing, means a commitment of one's whole life to the truth in which one believes. To believe in Jesus Christ, therefore, means that we live in such a way that our life would have no meaning if it were not for him. Let us examine more closely just what it means to believe.

Notes on the Text

v. 1ff   *Word*   In Greek Stoic philosophy the *logos* was the Universal Reason, divine but impersonal. Here John gives *logos* a distinct Christian content by showing that the Word was not only the eternal, personal God, but also that he became incarnate in Jesus. Cf. v. 14.

v. 11   *his own home*   Jesus was rejected by his hometown of Nazareth as well as his nation of Israel.

Comments and Questions for the Study

In this prologue to his Gospel, John has given a precise synthesis of the work and life of Jesus Christ. These few verses encompass a broad and profound content as they describe the greatness of Christ, the Verb or Word of God. They also mention John the Baptist, the forerunner of Christ. After reading the complete passage, we will focus our attention on vv. 10-13.

1. Read once again vv. 10-13.
   What persons or groups of persons do these verses speak about?
   Make a list of all that is said about each.
2. What incidents do you remember from the life of Jesus? The Gospels show him at a wedding, in the country, by the sea, in the temple, associating with the "undesirable elements" of society, with the poor. Think about all these scenes. Jesus was no monastic recluse, nor was he some philosopher cut off from contact with the world.
   "He was in the world" (v. 10). What does this phrase suggest?
   "The world was made through him. . ." (vv. 10-11). What relation between Jesus and the world do these verses establish?
3. In what sense did the world come to know Jesus (v. 10)?
   In what sense did it *not* know him?
   What do most people know about Jesus today? Do you think that they know what we have come to realise through this and previous studies?
   What do you know about Jesus?
4. "His own people received him not" (v. 11). How was this rejection shown? (Remember your previous studies)
5. To whom is v. 12 referring? Recall some examples of people who did receive Jesus. They lived with him, following him, listening to his teaching, obeying him and committing themselves to him. Observe that this verse identifies *receiving* him with *believing* in him.
   How do you receive a friend into your home? What is the difference between receiving a person and receiving an object?
   How does a man receive his wife, and a woman her husband, when they marry? (Marriage is a biblical picture of man's relation to Christ)
6. Read carefully this passage in which Jesus lays down the conditions for those who wish to receive him and follow him.
   "Now great multitudes accompanied him; and he turned and said to them, 'If any one comes to me and

does not hate his own father and mother and wife and children and brothers and sisters, yes, and even his own life, he cannot be my disciple. Whoever does not bear his own cross and come after me, cannot be my disciple. . . . So therefore, whoever of you does not renounce all that he has cannot be my disciple.' " *Luke 14:25-27, 33*

Jesus makes absolute demands, and receiving him means accepting them.

Have you received him? Have you let him become part of your life?

7. Let us now summarise briefly our five studies in order to place these demands in perspective: In our desire to run away from God (Study 1), we reject him and take the consequences of a sinful human condition (Study 2), thus becoming slaves to any one of a number of idols (Study 3). The way to be liberated is to *believe* in Jesus Christ, who brings about this spiritual revolution in our lives, the new birth (Study 4). Believing in Jesus, however, means accepting daily and unreservedly his conditions and demands.

Have you accepted him in this way?

8. V. 12 shows the result of this saving faith, which is the *power* to become children of God. To be a child means to be born into a family and to grow and develop your potential to become more and more like your father.

Relate v. 13 with the previous study (John 3:5-8). *Who alone can make us children of God?* Notice the emphasis laid upon the human impossibility of achieving this new birth. Your conversion to Christ and your transformation are the work of God. Your role is to believe and receive.

Summarise what vv. 10-13 say about Jesus Christ. What relation is there between believing and receiving? Explain briefly.

A Final Word

When you undertook this study, you were looking for something. Have you found it? Perhaps some of your discoveries have been surprising and disturbing. Perhaps you have changed some of your ideas, and although you haven't worked out the concepts clearly in your mind, the words of the Bible have made a decisive impact upon your life.

Why don't you try putting what you have learned into practice? You can stop trying to run away from God as you return to him and leave your idols behind. You can make a start on the road to true freedom and let Christ liberate you. You can allow the Spirit of God to accomplish the new birth in you and enable you to begin a new lifestyle.

As with all the important things in life, this is both simple and profound. Kneel down and talk to God. Speak to God, as you would to a person who you know is willing and happy to listen to you. Pray, telling Christ that you want to receive him as your Lord, that you repent of not having acknowledged him before and that you want to undertake the adventure of living as his disciple. Tell him that you accept his conditions, confident of his ability to transform you and make you faithful until the end. There are thousands of us who can assure you that you'll never regret your decision.

"Among these we all once lived in the passions of our flesh, following the desires of body and mind, and so we were by nature children of wrath, like the rest of mankind. But God, who is rich in mercy, out of the great love with which he loved us, even when we were dead through our trespasses, made us alive together with Christ (by grace you have been saved), and raised us up with him, and made us sit with him in the heavenly places in Christ Jesus, that in the coming ages he might show the immeasurable riches of his grace in kindness toward us in Christ Jesus." *Ephesians 2:3-7*

"For the wages of sin is death, but the free gift of God is eternal life in Christ Jesus our Lord." *Romans 6:23*

B Honest Answers to Honest Questions

We are living in an age of questionings. But often we find that the answers to these questions only raise other questions, and we are still dissatisfied.

In the New Testament we see people going with their questions to Jesus. And something very astonishing happened: Jesus did not only answer them, but in fact he solved the real problems of his inquirers, although often in an unexpected way.

Jesus answered people who were honest and open and who asked in sincerity. Many, however, came to him with dishonest questions to trap him or annoy him. Then Jesus answered in a different way. We invite you to be as honest as possible, as honest as the people we are going to look at. They are not different from us. Although from a different cultural and historical background, these people are all very human. They are one of us.

Therefore let us study these honest answers to honest questions to get help for our problems.

1 How Can We Know the Way?
John 14:1-14 (Thomas and Philip)

Context: The questions in this passage were raised by Jesus' own disciples during his last night with them before his death. They had been with him for about two years of intimate companionship and training. They were hand-picked men to whom Jesus was committing his world ministry after his death.

Notes on the Text

v. 2   *In my Father's house* Where Jesus came from and where he was returning to. "My Father" indicates their unique relationship.

v. 5   *Thomas* One of Jesus' chosen Twelve, often characterised by (healthy?) scepticism. See John 11:16, 20:24-25.

v. 6   *I am the way* May also imply "I will show you the way".

v. 8   *Philip* See John 1:46, 6:7, 12:22 for his pragmatic tendency.

v. 11   *the works* Jesus' many miracles of healing the sick, feeding the hungry and other demonstrations of his authority over life.

Questions for Study and Discussion

A.   Thomas: "How can we know the way?" vv. 1-7

1.   What is the logical connection between Jesus' words in v. 1 and v. 2? Why was it so important for Thomas to know where Jesus was going? What kind of answer might he have expected Jesus to give?

2. What are the various promises Jesus made to his disciples in this section?   To whom can they apply today?   In this context what did Jesus mean by "the way"?

B. Philip: "How can we see God?" vv. 8-11

3. Philip (and the others) did not understand fully what Jesus meant in v. 7. What seemed to puzzle him?
4. What do Jesus' questions in vv. 9-10 tell us about his reactions to Philip's request?   Do you think it was fair of Jesus to expect them to understand?   What are your reasons?
5. Did you notice Jesus' repetition of "believe . . . believe . . . believe"?   Why?   What did he say should be their basis of belief in him?

C. Jesus: "Believe in me" vv. 12-14

6. Does it surprise you that the disciples could still be confused about Jesus' real identity?   Yet how did Jesus show his confidence in them?   What did he mean by "greater works" in v. 12?
7. In vv. 13-14 Jesus clarifies the basis of this confidence. What is this basis?   How could this challenge them the very next day when Jesus their Master was to be crucified?

Practical Implications — Choose the applicable one.

a) Jesus — Who is he?   Are today's views of Jesus closer to his own statements about himself or to his disciples' views?
b) What do people today think is involved in following Jesus?   Compare this with what he says is implied in following him.
c) Can you identify with Thomas and Philip in this passage?   What is your first reaction to Jesus' answers, if you think of them as directed at you yourself?   Do you think this is an honest answer to an honest question?

2 Which Is the Greatest Commandment?
Mark 12:28-34 (A Teacher of the Law)

Context: This event occurred in Jerusalem during the last week before Jesus' death. The Jewish religious leaders had been asking many questions to try to trap him into saying something that could cause his arrest or ruin his popularity.

Notes on the Text

v. 28 *scribes* See Word List.

vv. 29-30 *Hear, O Israel* The creed of Israel usually recited twice daily by most scribes. See Dt. 6:4-5.

v. 30 *heart* See World List.

v. 31 This quotation is from Lv. 19:18.

v. 33 *whole burnt offerings* The Jewish sacrificial system was then still in operation, but the prophets had already shown that God preferred steadfast love to sacrifices, e.g., Ho 6:6.

v. 34 *the kingdom of God* See Word List.

Questions for Study and Discussion

A. A basic question, v. 28

1. What circumstances prompted the scribe to ask Jesus this question? Do you think his motive was, like the other scribes', to trap Jesus? Explain.

B. Jesus' dialogue with the scribe, vv. 29-33

2. What did Jesus mean by loving God with our heart, mind and strength? Discuss separately these various ways of loving, giving practical examples.

3. Why did Jesus put loving God first? What are the evidences that the scribe understood and agreed with Jesus?
4. Why is it more important to obey these commandments than to offer burnt offerings and sacrifices? On the other hand, what is the relation between these two expressions of worship of God?

C. Jesus' personal response to the scribe, v. 34

5. Seldom did Jesus evaluate individuals (as he did groups). What did Jesus see in this scribe that brought forth his positive evaluation?
6. Why did no one else dare ask Jesus any other question? What was it about Jesus that evidently impressed them?

Practical Implications — Choose the applicable one.

a) People today may not be sacrificing burnt offerings in order to rid themselves of guilt feelings. But they have different methods. How do we usually try to clear our conscience? How can this divert us from loving God and others?

b) Jesus said that the scribe was not far from the kingdom of God. What do you think he still lacked? How close to the kingdom are you?

3 How Often Shall I Forgive My Brother?
Matthew 18:21-35 (Simon Peter)

Context: Matthew has collected in Ch. 18 a series of Jesus' teaching on how brothers in his new kingdom should relate to one another. This was only a few months before his death in Jerusalem. Yet his own disciples were becoming more and more concerned with personal ambitions for the highest posts in his new messianic society. So Jesus had to stress the need for each to be humble and consider others as valuable brothers.

Notes on the Text

v. 22   *seven times* Symbolic, not literal meaning; Jesus may have been contrasting limitless mercy perhaps to Lamech's 490-fold revenge (Gn. 4:24).

v. 23   *kingdom of heaven* See Word List.
            servants Highly placed officials in the Emperor's service, who at times needed to borrow large sums from the imperial treasurer.

v. 24   *talent* See Word List.

v. 25   A way to deal with a debtor's default on debts was to sell him and his family into slavery.

v. 28   *denarius* See Word List.

Questions for Study and Discussion

A.   Peter's attitude, vv. 21-22

1.   Behind Peter's question in v. 21 was the Jewish teaching that a man need forgive another only up to three times. So then, what do you think was Peter's attitude here?

2.   If you had been Peter how would you have reacted to Jesus' reply?   Why do we find it difficult to forgive one another?

B. Jesus explains, vv. 23-35

3. Evidently Peter did not grasp Jesus' intention. So Jesus proceeded to elaborate his statement with a parable.
   What was your first reaction to the behaviour of the servant who forced his fellow servant to pay back his debt? Why?

4. Was the king's punishment of the servant justified? How so? Why ought the servant to have forgiven his fellow servant's debt?

5. Summarise the character of a) the king; b) the unforgiving servant.

C. Interpreting the parable, vv. 23-35

6. In this parable who does the king represent? Who do the servants represent? What does the servant's great debt to his lord represent?

7. How does this story answer Peter's question?

Practical Implications — Choose the applicable one.

a) The contrast between 10,000 talents and 100 denarii is very marked. What does this tell us about the way we react to everyday clashes and frictions?

b) What does it mean to forgive our brother "from the heart"? Who is our brother? What is our situation if we don't forgive a brother? Cf. Matthew 6:12-15.

c) What kind of debt do we owe to Christ? How can we repay it?

4 Then Who Can Be Saved?
Mark 10:23-31 (Peter)

Context: Jesus had just made clear to a rich youth the basis of obtaining eternal life: putting God first, not possessions. The young ruler failed this test, going away sad. Jesus took the immediate opportunity to drive the lesson home to his disciples, for these 12 men-in-training had witnessed the unusual encounter between Jesus and the rich youth.

Notes on the Text

vv. 23, 27 *looked* Lit. "gazing with keen attention".

v. 23 *kingdom of God* See Word List.

v. 24 *children* A master's affectionate term for his disciples. Jesus knew they had an immature view of riches and of God's salvation.

v. 25 *the eye of a needle* Possibly a pedestrians' tiny door cut into the huge city gate, or the whole verse is a familiar mid-east proverb.
camel The largest, clumsiest, and worst-tempered animal then.

v. 30 *age to come* See Word List.

Questions for Study and Discussion

A. Who can be saved? vv. 23-26

1. Why did Jesus say it was hard for a rich man to enter the kingdom of God? Was he against riches?
2. Note that twice Mark records the disciples were amazed at Jesus' firm statement about entering the kingdom of God. What does this indicate about their attitude to riches?

3. What emotional/mental response to Jesus' words do the men's words in v. 26 indicate? What seems to be their understanding of "saved"?

B. The impossible vs. the possible, v. 27

4. Jesus did not answer their question directly. But what are the clues to his thinking throughout the passage, including vv. 17-22?
   How does v. 27 climax Jesus' answer to his disciples?

C. Following Jesus all the way, vv. 28-31

5. Look at Peter's response to Jesus' answer. Perhaps his "we" was a self-conscious comparison to the rich man! What could he and the other disciples be feeling and thinking behind those words (v. 28)?
6. How literally do you think Jesus meant vv. 29-30? What, according to his words here, is the cost of discipleship?
7. On the other hand, what did he promise to those who follow him all the way?
   What illustration of this promise can you think of?

Practical Implications — Choose the applicable one.

a) What does it mean in our lives that God can do what we think is impossible? What does this tell us about God?
b) Contrast man's idea of salvation and Jesus' teaching on it. In what direct way does Jesus' teaching apply to us if we want salvation?

5   Who Are You, Jesus of Nazareth?
John 8:21-32 (Jews)

Context: Our passage continues Jesus' debate with the Jewish leaders in the storm centre of Jerusalem (See Ch. 8:12-20). The Pharisees were angered, but still unable to arrest him. However, some of them continued to listen with a genuine desire to know what kind of man Jesus of Nazareth was.

Notes on the Text

v. 21   *sin* Jesus links the word here with death. For sin is turning away from the source of life   from God himself, and thus leads to death.

v. 22   *the Jews* See Word List.

v. 23   *I am* Cf. vv. 24, 28. An expression for the eternally present tense and sovereignty of God. Jesus is claiming to be the Son of the One who revealed himself to Moses as "I am who (I say) I am" (Ex. 3:14).

v. 26   *true* What God the Father says and does is true. Light is in him, not in the world. In him only is ultimate truth.

v. 28   *Son of man* See Word List.
       lifted up Raised on the Roman cross of execution, but Jesus may also mean "exalted".

Questions for Study and Discussion

A.   You will die, vv. 21-24

1.   Look at the first part of this dialogue again. What coming event and its results was Jesus referring to? Why did the Jews not understand?

2. In what ways did Jesus possibly mean the Jews would "seek" him? In what way did they "die in their sin"?
3. What practical things may Jesus have had in mind when he said, "You are not of this world?" What are the indications that Jesus was not originally of this world?

B. **Who are you? vv. 25-27**

4. Note when the question in v. 25 appears in the whole debate. Why were the Jews asking this basic question only now? What does their question tell us about them?
    To what extent are Jesus' words in v. 26 an answer to their enquiry?

C. **You will know that I am he, vv. 28-32**

5. In v. 28 Jesus made clear that he knew they would kill him. What then could he have meant when he said that his death would reveal his real identity to them?
6. Throughout this debate Jesus' words reveal one strong frame of reference. From this, what details about his relationship to "the Father" do you learn?
    What do you think most impressed those who began to believe?
7. What did Jesus mean by "continue in my word"? How does the passage as a whole help you to understand the nature of the freedom about which Jesus speaks in v. 32?

Practical Implications — Choose the applicable one.

a) Think of some practical examples of the way we are bound to this world (mentally, physically, emotionally, consciously, unconsciously). How does this affect our view of Jesus Christ?
b) In what ways can we say that we too are crucifying Jesus in our day? What this reveal about our present "religion"?

6 Everyone Who Asks Receives
Luke 11:5-13

Context: Luke's gospel refers to Jesus' prayer life more often than any of the other gospels. Impressed by his praying habits, the disciples asked him to teach them how to pray. Jesus replied with the well-known "Lord's Prayer" (Lk. 11:1-4). Here Jesus uses the word "Abba" to address God, an Aramaic familiar form used by children when talking to their father. This way of speaking to God was new to the disciples. Jesus went on to illustrate the effects this personal, intimate relationship with God should have on his disciples' lives.

Notes on the Text

v. 5   *at midnight* In Palestine people often preferred to travel after dark rather than in the heat of the day.

v. 7   The house was probably a simple one-room home where the family all slept together — perhaps with the animals too! For the householder to answer the door would have meant disturbing the whole family.

v. 8   *importunity* Shameless persistence.

v. 13   *give the Holy Spirit* The Holy Spirit is the giver of gifts (1 Cor. 12:9-11)!

Questions for Study and Discussion

A.   Ask, seek, knock, vv. 5-10

1.   Every illustration has only one main point. What do you think is Jesus' main point in this parable for his disciples?

2.   Consider the situation in which the midnight caller found himself. On what did he rely when knocking at his neighbour's door? Why did he achieve his aim in the end? What would have resulted if he had given up?

3. "Ask", "seek" and "knock" are all continuous verbs; i.e., they imply a persistent action. What did Jesus say are the conditions for our asking something of God? How can we know we are asking for the right thing? What gives us the right to present our requests before God? Is there any reason why he might not answer us?

4. What attitude is implied by seeking and knocking? What is the promise for those who persist in these activities? Could there ever be a time when they are no longer necessary?

5. Consider the following statements of Jesus.
   "I am the door; if anyone enters by me he will be saved." (Jn. 10:9)
   "I am the way, the truth and the life. No one comes to the Father but by me." (Jn. 14:6)
   What relevance to the passage under study can you find?

B. Father and child, vv. 11-12

6. Jesus again reminded his disciples of the Father-love of God. What did he assume is the normal basis in the father-child relationship? What might be causes of fear and doubt in the child?

7. What are the similarities and differences between an earthly father and God as a Heavenly Father?

C. The Father's gift, v. 13

8. Jesus is concerned not only with man's physical needs; he is responding to man's spiritual hunger. How do you understand the Person and role of the Holy Spirit? Why is the Holy Spirit the gift God wants to give us? What difference should this gift make to our lives?

Practical Implications — Choose the applicable one.

a) Do you find it easy to think of God as your Father? What are the practical implications of doing so?
b) It is difficult to talk freely with someone you barely know. The more we get to know God, the easier it will be to pray to him. Has this been your experience?

39

A Final Word

As you have seen, Jesus' answers to human question often seem to be inadequate or strange at first sight. If we have a closer look and take time to think, we realise that they are very revealing. They do not only give the answer, but they also reveal something about both the question and the questioner.

Honest questions are asked by people who have a desire to know themselves as they really are. Take Job, for instance:

And the Lord said to Job: "Shall a faultfinder contend with the Almighty? He who argues with God, let him answer it". Then Job answered the Lord: "Behold, I am of small account; what shall I answer thee? I lay my hand on my mouth. I have spoken once, and I will not answer; twice, but I will proceed no further".

Than the Lord answered Job out of the whirlwind: "Gird up your loins like a man; I will question you, and you declare to me. Will you even put me in the wrong? Will you condemn me that you may be justified? Have you an arm like God, and can you thunder with a voice like his?" *Job 40:1-9*

Is it fair of God to challenge Job (man) like this? Compare this passage with the following one where Job answers God; it is his answer to God's answer:

I know that thou canst do all things, and that no purpose of thine can be thwarted. "Who is this that hides counsel without knowledge?" Therefore I have uttered what I did not understand, things too wonderful for me, which I did not know. "Hear, and I will speak; I will question you, and you declare to me." I had heard of thee by the hearing of the ear, but now my eye sees thee; therefore I despise myself, and repent in dust and ashes. *Job 42:1-6*

Has Job given up here? Is he accepting defeat? What insight has he received? Is his honesty real, or is it a way of escape? Can you see yourself in these words? What strikes you most?

Again, we can ask the question: Then who can be saved? Go back to Mark, chapter 10 which we studied, and now read verses 13-16:

And they were bringing children to him, that he might touch them; and the disciples rebuked them. But when Jesus saw it he was indignant, and said to them, "Let the children come to me, do not hinder them; for to such belongs the kingdom of God. Truly, I say to you, whoever does not receive the kingdom of God like a child shall not enter it." And he took them in his arms and blessed them, laying his hands upon them.

Verse 15 is the key verse. "Truly, I say to you, whoever does not receive the kingdom of God like a child shall not enter it." In what way do we have to become like children? Is this passage a little simplistic? Or is it thoroughly radical?

The Bible not only answers human questions, but returns the questions in another form to us. Then it is up to us, up to you, to answer.

C I Believe; Help My Unbelief!

Unbelief has many faces. Sometimes it has a hard face, and at other times it has a desperate one. Sometimes it has a naive face, and at other times it has a self-righteous one. Sometimes it has an honest face, and at other times it has a dishonest face.

When Jesus was on earth, he met people with different problems of faith. He never "gave" the same answers to them. Rather he related to each individual on his or her level of understanding. But always he sought to move the person from that level, building up faith in himself and in the eternal values of God's kingdom.

The selected passages are again in topical order. The first four are concerned with men or women who were in desperate need — their own misery or their loved ones' suffering. In Studies 5 and 6 we are in the presence of educated people and community leaders. Their responses to Jesus Christ have importance because of their influential position. The last three studies show us the honest reactions of Jesus' closest disciples.

(These studies were originally prepared by some GBU student leaders in France. They were compiled under the title *Je Crois; Viens au Secours du Mon Incredulite!* Later they were translated and adapted for Asian students).

43

1 A Desperate Father
Mark 9:14-29

Background: Jesus has just been transfigured on the mountain before his three closest disciples. For him the transfiguration (Gk: *metamorphosis*) is confirmation of his mission from God as he faces the cross. The disciples, however, are still in a daze after this spectacular event, and Jesus has to awaken them. He knows that they must confront human misery on their return to the valley of daily life.

Notes on the Text

v. 14 *disciples* The nine others left in the valley.
scribes See Word List.

v. 15 *greatly amazed* Perhaps at an afterglow of his transfiguration.

v. 17 *dumb, unclean spirit* Cf. v. 25. The NT recognises demon possession as a fact which is only now beginning to be acknowledged again in the west.

v. 18 Cf. vv. 20, 22. Symptoms of extreme epilepsy.

v. 29 *prayer and fasting* Cf. Mt. 6:5-18, where Jesus commends them as sincere means by which to draw near to God, not as showy rituals.

Development

A. The situation: a picture of humanity, vv. 14-16

1. What a contrast between the group from the mountain top and the group in the valley! Based on vv. 14-15 what difference do you see?

2. How would you characterise each of the three subgroups in the valley? What seems to be the main concern of each group? How does each apparently regard the pitiable situation of the child?
In what ways does the child symbolise our human situation today?

B. The father: belief and unbelief, vv. 17-24

3. The dialogue between the father and Jesus is one of the most dramatic in the gospels. Imagine yourself in the father's mental/emotional state. Observe his words closely. What does he expect when he first comes with his young son? What is his attitude to the child's condition?
4. What is his regard for Jesus? How does he show faith in him? How does he show unbelief? Why is he struggling? What similarities between him and yourself do you see?

C. The disciples: a setback, vv. 14-18, 28-29

5. What is their part throughout the event? Why are they unable to heal the child? (Don't judge superficially, but stick to the text!)
6. What does v. 28 especially tell us about the progress of their faith in Jesus? What kind of Christians might they represent?

D. Jesus: faith and prayer

7. Notice how he deals with each group. On this basis, what would you say is his opinion of each? What deeply disturbs him? Why do you think his feelings are so strong?
8. What important lessons is he teaching these people? Why?

Practical Reflection — Choose the one most applicable.

a) If prayer is talking with the Lord Jesus, then what can we learn about praying from the father and from the disciples?
b) How is man's attitude towards evil powers characterised nowadays? What is Jesus' attitude?
c) The father had conflicting feelings and beliefs with regard to Jesus' power, and yet he finally looked to him for help. What can we learn from him?

2 A Persistent Mother

Matthew 15:21-28

Background: Jesus has withdrawn to foreign territory, NW of Palestine 1) to let the hot controversy with the Jerusalem investigation committee cool down, and 2) to rest and instruct his disciples in privacy (Mk. 7:24).

Notes on the Text

v. 21 *Tyre and Sidon* Towns of non-Jewish Phoenecia, two days journey (50 miles) from Galilee. The major religion was worship of a moon goddess.

v. 22 *Canaanite* A foreigner, considered a lowly pagan by the Jews.
Son of David See Word List.

v. 26 *the dogs* "Pet dog" (Gk), so an uncomplimentary but not derogatory term. Jesus is not stressing the fact of being a dog, but the difference between pet dogs and children.

Development

A.   In pagan territory, vv. 21-22

1.   The writer Matthew makes clear the unusual circumstances of this event. How does he do this?
2.   What else about this woman makes the situation even more unusual?   For instance, what titles does she use in addressing Jesus?

B.   Strange interaction, vv. 22-28

3.   If you were reading this story for the first time, what would be your impressions of Jesus?   On what do you base these impressions?
4.   Let's suspend judgment on him till we have taken a closer look at the woman. The character of the woman gradually emerges. What quality of character do you see at each step of her encounter with Jesus?

C.   The disciples' reaction, vv. 23-24

5.   How do they regard the woman?   Examine Jesus' statement in v. 24. In what way could this be an answer to their proposed solution?
     What do they not see in the woman and in the encounter that Jesus sees?

D.   Jesus her Lord, vv. 23-28

6.   Examine the ways in which Jesus responds to the woman. Why is he silent at first?   What can silence mean in different situations?
7.   Finally he speaks directly to her (v. 26). But why does he use words that sound like rejection and even insult?
     If he had granted her request at the beginning, what would he have accomplished?   What is he teaching her? His disciples?

Practical Reflection — Choose the one most applicable.

a)   Is humility a necessary aspect of faith?   Explain your view. How does the woman's humility differ from some of our ideas about humility?
b)   Is it for God's pleasure that the way of faith is often costly?   If not, what are possible reasons?
c)   What do you feel most desperate or frustrated about? Compare your situation with the woman's. Can you imagine yourself going to a man like Jesus as the woman did?   What kind of thing must first happen in your life for you to take that step?

3 An Army Officer Who Amazed Jesus
Luke 7:1-10

Background: As the crowds from both Palestine and Phoenecia increase, Jesus chooses twelve special companions and co-workers from among the serious disciples. After more public teaching, he returns to Capernaum, his adopted hometown, as well as his base of operations. It is here that Jesus has also healed an official's son without seeing him (John 4:46-54).

Notes on the Text

v. 2   *centurion*   Equivalent to an army captain, in charge of 100 men. This one is in the Roman occupation army in Palestine.

v. 3   *elders of the Jews*   See "ruler" in Word List.

v. 7   *my servant*   The centurion himself does not use "slave", but *pais* (Gk), indicating an assistant who is a young man.

v. 8   *under authority*   Under superior officers and ultimately under the Roman emperor, whom he probably never saw or ever would see.

v. 9   *marvel*   Not "was surprised", but "contemplated with wonder". Only here and in Mk. 6:6 is it recorded that Jesus "marvelled".

Development

A.   Luke's description of the man, vv. 1-3

1.   Luke, a Gentile himself, always takes a special interest in other Gentiles who believe in Jesus. How does he introduce this one in the narrative? What facts about the centurion's character are implied here?

B. The elder's opinion of him, vv. 4-5

2. What is the centurion's relationship to the Jewish elders?
   What specific opinion of him do they convey to Jesus, both by what they say and the way they approach Jesus?

C. The centurion's self-appraisal, vv. 6-8

3. Luke now gives a greater proportion of his narrative to the man's appraisal of himself. How does it compare with the elders' opinion?
4. In what ways does he demonstrate his sincerity about not being worthy of Jesus' presence?
   Most of us have probably had feelings of unworthiness in the presence of certain people. Would you say your feelings were the same as or different from the centurion's feeling?   Please explain.
5. What do the centurion's words in v. 8 tell us about his view of Jesus?

D. Jesus' evaluation of him, vv. 9-10

6. How do you picture Jesus' reaction to the centurion's message?   What does Jesus recognise as unique in his faith?
   What indications in v. 9 show he wants the crowd also to recognise the man's unique faith?
7. Why is Jesus' praise of the man also touched with sadness?

Practical Reflection — Choose the one most applicable.

a) What is the relationship between authority and faith? For instance, what kind of leader do we trust?   Why?
b) What might arouse us to faith in God?   If you find it difficult to believe in the way the army officer did, try to think what makes you reluctant, and discuss it openly in the group.

4 A Criminal's Last Minute Pardon
Luke 23:32-43

Background: Jesus has arrived at the place of execution for criminals. Having dragged his cross with the help of Simon of Cyrene from the city to the hill, he is nailed to the cross by a squad of Roman soldiers. Also present are the religious officials and a mixed crowd of curious/awed/sad/mocking bystanders. It is about mid-day.

Notes on the Text

v. 32   *two criminals* Mt. 27:38 and Mk. 15:27 say "thieves", "brigands".

v. 33   *The Skull* Hebrew = Golgotha; Latin = Calvary.

v. 34   *divided his clothes* Customary right of executors. See Ps. 22:16-18.

v. 36   *vinegar* Beverage containing soporific drug.

v. 39   *railed or insulted* Matthew and Mark record that both criminals did, indicating that one later changed his attitude.

v. 43   *Paradise* A Persian word referring to a beautiful park. Jews believed it (= Sheol or Hades) was a resting place before the final judgment.

Development

A.   Three criminally condemned men, v. 32

1.   Outwardly Jesus is no different from the other men dragging their crosses. They have all been condemned as criminals. Apart from this passage we know nothing about the two others. But what can we try to understand about them from our knowledge of them as "thieves"? (See note above)

B. What the two saw and heard, vv. 33-38

2. The two thieves began the same way but ended differently. Let's see why. Who apparently is the first of the three to be nailed to his cross? What effect does this have on the others?
3. Now the two can hear and see Jesus as he responds to the execution. What do you think they learn about him?

C. Difference in their final response, vv. 39-41

4. One thief is reviling Jesus. Is this mere provocation? Does he expect a miraculous act of salvation?
5. Obviously something revolutionary has happened in the second thief while he has been watching and listening to Jesus. Analyse his words. How does he basically see Jesus?

D. The king on the cross, vv. 42-43

6. In these two verses are two very remarkable statements. Let us first examine the one by the nameless thief. What does each word/phrase reveal about the radical change in him? What is now his clearest concept about Jesus?
7. Jesus' personal response to him is equally radical. What does it tell us a) about his regard for this fellow criminal? b) about himself? c) about the basis of personal salvation?

Practical Reflection — Choose the one most applicable.

a) Considering the attitude of the soldiers and the first criminal, what would you expect a "messiah" to do in these circumstances? What actually happened?
b) How would you describe a "conversion" on the basis of this passage? Is there anything which strikes you as being similar to your own situation?

5 Simon the Pharisee, a Suspicious Host
Luke 7:36-50

Background: Jesus' popularity and growing disciples are certainly being noted by the religious establishment. As a whole these leaders are very hostile (Luke 7:29-30). But some begin seriously to consider the validity of Jesus' claims. Simon seems to be one.

Notes on the Text

v. 36   *sit at the table*   Probably in the more informal eating area of the courtyard which the woman can easily enter.

v. 37   *sinner*   Luke's term for a prostitute.
alabaster flask of ointment   The costly spikenard from N. India.

v. 40   *Simon*   One of the three or four Pharisees actually named in the Bible, possibly indicating that he became a believer.

v. 44   *water for my feet*   A host's minimum courtesy to his dusty guests.

v. 47   *are forgiven*   The imperfect past tense reads more clearly as "have been forgiven" (i.e., in a previous meeting).

Development

A.   Simon the Pharisee: the struggle to believe

1.   What are your first impressions of Simon?
What are possible reasons that Simon invites Jesus to dinner?   Why doesn't he extend to Jesus the usual courtesies of a host?

2.   Simon obviously has a double reaction − to the woman's behaviour and to Jesus' attitude to her. Whose behaviour disturbs him most?

What does this reaction reveal about his past views of Jesus?   What does it also reveal about his probable views of "holiness"?

3. On the other hand, do you see any clues to his possible openness to Jesus?

B.   The woman: the boldness to thank

4. What gives her boldness to enter a Pharisee's house — uninvited?   What is her only concern?   In what ways does she demonstrate this?
What does Jesus see in her that Simon does not?

5. What difference do you see in the woman's attitude towards herself and Simon's attitude towards himself?

C.   Jesus: ways of communicating

6. What do you think Jesus' calm acceptance of the woman's behaviour and her gifts communicate to her — and to the others watching?

7. What is Jesus essentially saying to Simon in his short parable?   Why does he use it?   How does he repeat his message?
What positive things does he see and appeal to in Simon?   What are the most important things he wants Simon to know?

8. Summarise Jesus' ways of relating to Simon and to the woman. What do you consider most outstanding about Jesus in this event?

Practical Reflection — Choose the one most applicable.

a) What do people usually mean by "respectable sins"? What do you think Jesus would say about this?

b) Note that Jesus is master of this unusual situation and that he is able to use these otherwise disruptive incidents to teach. Imagine yourself as one of the guests watching things from beginning to end. How would your opinion of the woman and of Simon be changed? How could it affect your attitude to your own situation?

6 A Dissatisfied Rich Young Man
Mark 10:17-27

Background: Jesus is in Perea (modern Transjordan) on his way to Jerusalem (v. 32), where he faces certain death. A very enthusiastic crowd follows him. But he is not deceived by their superficiality. Rather he keeps teaching in clear terms that there is a price to pay if they genuinely wish to follow him.

Notes on the Text

v. 17 Mt. 19:22 says this man is young. Lk. 18:18 says he is a ruler. All three accounts say he is rich.

v. 24 *amazed* It was common OT belief that riches were God's rewards.

v. 25 *the eye of a needle* Possibly the huge door into a typical mid-east city had a small door through which people could walk, but not camels.

Development

A. The young man: all eagerness, vv. 17-22

1. What is the young man's idea of goodness? What does Jesus say about it? Is Jesus denying his deity in v. 18? What seems to be the man's concept of salvation?

2. In what direction does he gradually move in the course of his interview with Jesus? Why does he finally go away sad?

B.   **Jesus: all love, vv. 17-22**

3.   What basic error does Jesus detect in the young man's thinking about salvation?
4.   He begins to correct this error by referring to the basic commandments (Ex. 20).
     Which of the Ten Commandments does he omit?   Why do you think he omits them?
5.   Notice at what point in the conversation Mark mentions Jesus' spontaneous response to the young man. Why at this point?   What does it tell us about Jesus?
6.   How do you interpret Jesus' words in v. 21, especially as addressed to this man?   Why does Jesus demand so much of him?
     What is the underlying principle applying to us today?

C.   **The disciples: all amazement, vv. 23-27**

7.   The disciples have been witnessing this encounter with keen interest. What new teaching of Jesus amazes (shocks) them?   What does this reveal about their ideas regarding riches?   Regarding the basis for salvation?
8.   Summarise what the disciples learned about eternal salvation that day.

Practical Reflection — Choose the one most applicable.

a)   If God is the giver of all things, then why is it difficult to enter the kingdom of God with riches?
b)   Do Jesus' words sound discouraging to you?   What does Jesus want to do in us?
c)   The young man needed to repent from his love of riches. What may we need to repent from if we really want eternal life?

Nathanael a Prejudiced Israelite
John 1:43-51

Background: After his baptism and 40 days of temptations in the desert, Jesus begins his public ministry. He meets his first disciples from those who have been touched with the message of repentance by John the Baptist. These first encounters are near the Jordan River, where John has been preaching and baptising. Then Jesus returns to his home province of Galilee.

Notes on the Text

v. 45 *Nathanael* Cf. Jn 21:2; "Bartholomew" in Mk. 3:18, Mt. 10:3.

v. 46 *Nazareth* See Word List.

v. 47 *guile* Deceit, duplicity, trickery.

v. 50 *fig tree* A favourite place for rest, meditation; possibly a figurative term for study of the OT law at home.

vv. 47-51 Jesus is thinking about the history of Jacob ("supplanter"), whose name was later changed to Israel ("prince with God"). See Gn. 28:12 and 32:28.

Development

A. Initial reaction, vv. 43-47a vv. 43-47a

1. Nathanael first hears about Jesus in a positive witness from his friend Philip. But his reaction is negative! On what does he base his obvious prejudice against Jesus?

2. In what way is Philip instrumental in Nathanael's encounter with the Son of God?

B.   Encounter with Jesus, vv. 47-49

3.   Why do you think Jesus describes him as "an Israelite without guile"?   What proves this description of Nathanael later on?
4.   What about Jesus most impresses Nathanael?   Note his titles for Jesus. What would a keen OT student like Nathanael mean in using them?
Why could he change his mind about Jesus after his first prejudice?
5.   What can we learn about Jesus in the way he made personal contact with a prejudiced Bible scholar?

C.   Basis for belief, vv. 50-51

6.   Jesus himself is not as easily impressed by Nathanael's quick belief! How does he evaluate Nathanael's belief at this point?
7.   How does he then proceed to help Nathanael build a solid basis for faith in him?   What various things does he promise Nathanael?
Since Nathanael is very familiar with the implications of the OT story of Jacob, what could these promises mean to him?
8.   Summarise Nathanael's growth in faith in this passage. What does he begin with and what does he end with?

Practical Reflection — Choose the one most applicable.

a)   What are common prejudices against Jesus today? What do prejudices often hide?   How can they trap us?
b)   Consider the way both Philip and Jesus met Nathanael's arguments. What can we learn from them?
c)   Do you understand why such an apparently minor incident as Jesus' knowledge of Nathanael sitting under the fig tree should arouse such an exclamation from Nathanael (v. 49)?   Suggest reasons.

8 The Disciples in a Panic
Mark 4:35-41

Background: Jesus has had a long day, publicly teaching the crowd and privately explaining to his disciples. Now he deliberately leaves the crowd, and with his disciples proceeds to the region on the east coast of Lake Galilee. Suddenly another crisis arises.

Notes on the Text

v. 36   *other boats*   They were also crossing, but the event is from the viewpoint of those on the main boat.

v. 37   See "Galilee" in Word List.

v. 39   *Be still*   Literally *"Be muzzled!"*; same as in Mk. 1:25.

v. 40   *afraid*   "Timid". Cf. v. 41, "filled with awe" or literally "to fear with a great fear".

Development

A.   The disciples' reactions, vv. 35-38

1.   Consider what has happened on "that day". How do you think Jesus and his disciples feel at this time? For what possible reasons does Jesus suggest going to the other side?

2.   Some of these disciples are experienced fishermen in this lake. Yet what chain of reactions to the sudden storm do you observe in them?
What seems to underlie their question to Jesus? From their viewpoint how justified is this reaction to him?

B. Jesus' calm control, v. 39-41

3. What possible reason is there for Jesus' being able to
    sleep in the midst of a frightening storm and overwhelm-
    ing need?
    As you see Jesus sleeping and later controlling the
    storm, what do you learn about him?
4. Jesus' questions reveal his intentions for his men-in-
    training. If Jesus is testing them (as he often did), what
    is the value of this particular experience?   What else
    does he want to teach?
5. The story ends with one of the most important ques-
    tions the disciples ever asked. What does it imply about
    their past belief in Jesus?
    What does it tell us of what they have just learned about
    him?
    What does it tell us of their attitude towards nature?
    What does it hint about their future regard for him?

Practical Reflection — Choose the one most applicable.

a) Are human circumstances blind, the result of chance?
    Explain your view.
b) Compare Jesus' sleeping here with his silent response to
    the Syrophoenecian woman (Mt. 15:21-28). What can
    God's silences teach us?
c) We think we can handle life by ourselves — until a crisis
    arises. What can the disciples' experience teach us?

Background: Three days after Jesus dies, various people begin to report they have seen him. The hearers react differently. John 20:1-31 describes three interesting interviews with Jesus — Mary Magdalene, the ten disciples and Thomas. Here we concentrate on the one with Thomas.

Notes on the Text

v. 24   *Thomas* Cf. John 11:16 and 14:5, which also reveal scepticism.

v. 25   Luke 24:36-43 has a fuller account of this appearance of Jesus.

v. 26   *the house* Perhaps the same upper room as in Mk. 14:15.

       doors were shut Jesus' new body apparently could penetrate matter.

v. 27   *Do not be faithless* is better translated "Do not be unbelieving."

Development

A.   Thomas: psychological condition, vv. 24-25

1.   What are possible reasons that Thomas was absent from the first meeting with Jesus? On what do the other disciples base their faith?

2.   Do you think Thomas completely rejects the possibility that Jesus is alive? Explain your view.
   What is the positive side of Thomas' demand for visible, physical proof? Can you blame him for this? Give your reasons.

3. Think of the choice Thomas makes when he doubts Jesus. What risks is he taking for himself and his future?

B. **Jesus: personal encounter, vv. 26-27**

4. Note that Jesus has a true understanding of Thomas' doubts. How does he show that he understands him? What does he emphasise to Thomas? Why do you think Jesus makes this special effort to meet Thomas?

C. **Thomas' confession of faith, v. 28**

5. Let's look at Thomas' confession of faith. Remembering his background as a disciple, what do you think he means by his exclamation? (*Note:* Thomas is the first disciple to call Jesus his God!)
According to what you understand of Thomas' character, do you think this is a sudden, impulsive confession?

D. **Jesus' response to Thomas, vv. 29-31**

6. Jesus' response to Thomas' confession is mixed. In what ways is it a reproach? In what ways is it a promise?
7. What deeper lessons of faith does Jesus want to teach Thomas — and us?
8. The author John then concludes the main body of his book (Ch. 21 is an epilogue) with an appeal to his readers.
Since people today do not see the physically resurrected Jesus as Thomas did, how can they just as fully believe him?

Practical Reflection — Choose the one most applicable.

a) What is good about doubt? When is it foolish? What is the relation of doubt to honesty? The relation of doubt to faith? What different kinds of doubt exist?
b) What encourages faith? What can rescue us from doubts?
c) Can you identify with Thomas? In what respect?

A Final Word

Kierkegaard: "Also, from a spiritual point of view there comes a time when we feel totally inadequate; when we emerge naked from our self-inspection, as in the beginning from the body of our mother
and then, with deep sorrow, like Adam we must say: 'I heard the sound of thee in the garden, and I was afraid, because I was naked; and I hid myself'.
but this is necessary, in order that God can create something out of us; for God always creates out of nothing, and He does not need substance or our human wisdom." *Journal*

[14] For the love of Christ controls us, because we are convinced that one has died for all; therefore all have died. [15] And he died for all, that those who live might live no longer for themselves but for him who for their sake died and was raised. [16] From now on, therefore, we regard no one from a human point of view; even though we once regarded Christ from a human point of view, we regard him thus no longer. [17] Therefore, if any one is in Christ, he is a new creation; the old has passed away, behold, the new has come. [18] All this is from God, who through Christ reconciled us to himself and gave us the ministry of reconciliation; [19] that is, God was in Christ reconciling the world to himself, not counting their trespasses against them and entrusting to us the message of reconciliation. [20] So we are ambassadors for Christ, God making his appeal through us. We beseech you on behalf of Christ, be reconciled to God. [21] For our sake he made him to be sin who knew no sin, so that in him we might become the righteousness of God.
[1] Working together with him, then, we entreat you not to accept the grace of God in vain. For he says, [2] "At the acceptable time I have listened to you, and helped you on the day of salvation." Behold, now is the acceptable time; behold, now is the day of salvation. *II Cor. 5:14-6:2*

1. Discuss from this passage the meaning of dying and living.
2. Why is death a prerequisite to life?   Why did one have to die for all?   What is the meaning of "being in Christ" and of "reconciliation"?

3. To live for myself means to believe in myself. To be honest with myself means no longer being able to live for myself. What does it mean to live for Christ? (v. 15)
4. II Cor. 5:20-6:2 is an appeal to us —
   a) "to be reconciled to God". What kind of answer and action does Paul expect from us?
   b) "not to accept the grace of God in vain". When will God's grace be effective in us? In what ways will it affect our lives? (To answer this last question go back again to vv. 14-17 and discuss these verses one by one)

Part II

Who Then Is Jesus Christ?

In the second part of this book, the emphasis is on the character and mission of Jesus Christ. The question we want to ask ourselves is, who is he?

Was Jesus a philosopher like Socrates? An ethical teacher like Confucius? A moral example like Buddha? Or was he a revolutionary, a Camillo Torres? Was he perhaps a very intelligent man who has deceived us all by his clever thinking, but who himself suffered from an awareness of the vanity of all things and all thought? Or was his life a tragic failure of which his early death was just an indication? Is he one of the thousand-and-one "avatars", of which we are beginning to grow tired in our modern world? An enemy of the people? An intruder into my smoothly-running private life?

Many people make a quick judgment about his identity, but have never actually read in depth the story of his life. This is what we are inviting you to do in the following studies.

D Jesus: Man and Saviour

"What is this? A new teaching! He speaks with authority, not like our religious leaders!" "He's mad. Put him away!" "And all spoke well of him, and wondered at (his) gracious words." "He's demon-possessed. Silence him!" "We never saw anything like this!" "He's nothing but a peasant carpenter. Ignore him!" "Come, see a man who told me all that I ever did. Can this be the Messiah?" "He's a blasphemer. Destroy him!"

"A great prophet has risen among us. God has visited his people!" "He's a provincial agitator. Get rid of him!" "We can't arrest him. No man ever spoke like this man!" "Let's make him king!" "He's a political traitor. Kill him!" "Take him yourselves and crucify him. I find no crime in him." "Truly this was the Son of God!"

And the controversy has continued to rage on from that day to this. Jesus Christ was nothing, if not controversial. How could one man — a young one, too — call forth such contradictory and impassioned opinions? Who was he? What was he really like? Why was he so controversial? Where did the controversy lead him to? Did he consider it worthwhile?

Men and women argue, debate, opinionate and sentimentalise about Jesus Christ. But not many take the time and effort to investigate the historical facts about his person and his mission. This series can help you to examine the primary documents on his life so you can intelligently answer these crucial questions about the Man who claimed to be the Saviour of the World.

1 Jesus Is Tempted As One of Us
Luke 4:1-12

Context: Jesus, like his fellow Jews, was baptised by John the Baptist in the river Jordan, fully identifying with his people. He was one of us, so in spite of his purity and integrity he underwent baptism as a sign of man's need for repentance and forgiveness, and as a commitment to a new way of living. He was an example and forerunner, a teacher and representative. God endowed him with his Holy Spirit, then led him into the desert for still another kind of preparation for his life work.

Notes on the Text

v. 2 *forty days* The many biblical references to the number forty indicates a fulness of time, often to test, purify and prepare people for a new development in the history of God's mighty acts on man's behalf, e.g., Noah, Moses, Israel in the wilderness, Elijah.

v. 5 *devil* See Word List.
took him up Mt. 4:8 says it was to "a very high mountain", but either description can refer to a keen appeal to Jesus' imagination.

v. 4 Cf. vv. 8, 12, where Jesus also quotes from the OT, Dt. 8:3, 6:13, 6:16.

Development of Study/Discussion Questions

A. Instant satisfaction? vv. 1-4

1. What do you imagine the effect on a man would be after such a long period of fasting and solitariness?
2. Note the contrast between the Spirit, who indwelt Jesus and the devil, an external power, eager to penetrate into

68

his mind and heart. Compare this event with another great human battle in early history, in Paradise between Adam and Eve and the devil (Gn. 3:1-8).

What similarities do you notice between the devil's words to Jesus and his words to Eve? And what might the subtle differences in his words reveal? In both cases what did the devil basically try to achieve?

B. **Instant achievements? vv. 5-8**

3. Ultimately God would glorify Jesus Christ as his Son and make him King of the earth. This is what the devil said he could make him as well. But what are the differences between God's way and the devil's way, as Jesus himself suggested?

C. **Instant popularity? vv. 9-12**

4. What do you think made this last temptation so difficult to resist? What human weakness was the devil trying to exploit here?

5. The devil quoted scripture correctly (Ps. 91:11-12), but why was this quotation misapplied?

   Why was Jesus' answer rightly applied? (Dt. 6:16)

D. **Summary:** What similarities can you find in all three attacks of the devil? What similarities do you discover in the ways Jesus resisted him? What do you see as the main outcome of Jesus' resistance?

Practical Themes — Choose the appropriate one.

a) In which way are Jesus' three temptations like the ones we generally face? Do you recognise yourself in Jesus here?

b) What does Jesus' use of scripture teach us about answering the devil's attacks? How can we begin to know and use it as well as he did?

2 Jesus Defies Tradition
Luke 13:10-17

Context: Jesus was going to Jerusalem with his disciples for the last time. The hostility of the scribes and Pharisees had hardened into schemes to destroy him (11:53-54). This contrasted with his great popularity with the common people (12:1). The present event shows this striking contrast.

Notes on the Text

v. 11 *spirit of infirmity* Cf. v. 16. Jesus sees not only human sin but also human suffering as due ultimately to Satan.

v. 12 *Woman* See Word List.

v. 14 *ruler of the synagogue* Leading officer who presided at the worship and maintained order and proprieties. Cf. Acts 13:15.

v. 15 *hypocrites* "Play-actors" (Gk), as in the theatre.

v. 16 *daughter of Abraham* A Jewess, a member of God's family.

Development of Study/Discussion Questions

A. The Woman's hopeless condition, vv. 10-11

1. What does the text clearly tell us about the woman? What does it indirectly tell us about her?

B. Jesus' response to the woman, vv. 12-13

2. Try to picture Jesus' teaching the congregation — then noticing her among the people. From what followed, and what he later said in v. 16, how do you suppose he felt when he saw her?
3. Luke the writer was a physician who was always interested in the *way* Jesus healed people. What interesting details did he record?
   What do you think he wanted to tell us about Jesus?

C. The ruler's indignation, v. 14

4. What contrast does "but" in v. 14 introduce?
   From this what do we learn about the ruler's religious values?

D. Jesus' response to the ruler, vv. 15-17

5. Note how Luke consciously or unconsciously changed Jesus' title in v. 15. In what ways did Jesus' response to the ruler and his group (cf. v. 16) indeed demonstrate his complete mastery over the situation?
6. With only two questions Jesus taught some fundamental truth about people. What was his evaluation of his adversaries? of the woman? of human suffering?
7. How was Jesus' religion radically different from that of his enemies?

Practical Themes — Choose the appropriate one.

a) What do we learn from this passage about the use of the law? Why do we so easily fall into the trap of legalism?
b) How can we develop Jesus' sensitive compassion to needy people around us?

71

3 Jesus Predicts His Death & Resurrection
Luke 9:18-27

Context: This passage comes after Jesus had fed 5000 hungry people in the wilderness. It was one of the greatest and clearest miracles he performed because so many experienced it. His disciples, who had now followed Jesus for almost two years, were thus in a better position to consider who Jesus really was. It is followed by the transfiguration, his highest human experience when God clearly confirmed his death mission to both Jesus and his disciples.

Notes on the Text

v. 19   *John the Baptist, Elijah....* The Jews expected certain great prophets of the past to reappear just before the Messiah himself would come.

v. 20   *Christ* See "Messiah" in Word List.

v. 22   *Son of man* See Word List.

v. 23   *take up his cross* Picture of a condemned criminal on his way to execution. The disciples must have been shocked, for they knew very well that the cross did not simply represent a burden, but something which led inevitably to death.

v. 24   *would save his life* Though Jesus is making a word-play on "life", he is also emphasising "would" ("will", "determine").

v. 27   *kingdom of God* See Word List.

Development of Study/Discussion Questions

A.   A crucial interview, vv. 18-20

1.   Mt. 16:13 says they were in the region of Caesarea Philippi, a heathen place, but private enough to be alone with his disciples, away from the hostile leaders and pressing crowds. Compare who the people said that Jesus was with what Peter said.
   What made the difference between public opinion and Peter's confession?

B. Prediction of his passion, vv. 21-22

2. Why do you think Jesus forbade them to tell people he was the "anointed one"?

3. The early stages of Jesus' ministry were marked by great popularity. So, if you put yourself in the place of the disciples, why would Jesus' words in vv. 21-22 be startling? (How would you respond to his strict prohibition? to his predictions?)

4. What threat did Jesus' teaching present to the Jewish religious leaders? What do we learn about these people from their reaction to Jesus?

C. Jesus' definition of discipleship, vv. 23-27

5. Jesus' next words are on the meaning of true discipleship. What connection do you see between this topic and the discussion in vv. 18-22? What are the different things he said about discipleship under him? Which part do you find difficult to understand?

6. What could Jesus possibly mean by "taking up your cross daily"? Jesus' words in v. 24 seem quite contrary to our way of life and thinking. What assumptions about human nature was Jesus making here?

7. Consider the meaning of "being ashamed" in v. 26. What is its significance for us today?

Practical Themes — Choose the appropriate one.

a) Jesus called himself the "Son of man", and as such is the model of a true human being. Do you think the kind of life he was living was truly human?

b) Discuss some modern ideas of what a "Messiah" should be. Compare these with Jesus' way of life. How are they similar or different?

c) In what practical ways do we all try and "save our lives"? What precisely does Jesus mean by "losing our lives for his sake"?

4 Jesus Seeks & Saves Zaccheus
Luke 19:1-10

Context: Zaccheus was one of the last individuals Jesus personally encountered before reaching Jerusalem and his death. Luke evidently included him as a clear illustration not only of Jesus' way of relating to people, but also of his mission on earth. This mission became more sharply focused with each mile closer to Jerusalem's hostile religious leaders.

Notes on the Text

v. 1   *Jericho*   See Word List.

v. 2   *Zaccheus*   A Hebrew word meaning "pure".

v. 4   *sycamore*   A roadside tree related to the mulberry, easy to climb.

v. 9   *son of Abraham*   A true Jew, a member of God's family, who understands the spiritual values of God's kingdom.

Development of Study/Discussion Questions

A.   The city and the man, vv. 1-4, 7

1.   The note above on Jericho should help us to understand our main character. How does it broaden your understanding of Zaccheus?   a) his background?   b) his social standing?   c) his character with its good and bad traits?

B. The man and Jesus, vv. 5-9

2. If you knew nothing about Jesus and came upon this story only now, what impressions would you have of him up to v. 5? Jesus did not rebuke or criticise Zaccheus, but approached him as a friend. Can you understand why the people resented this?
Think of the kind of people you really despise. How would you react to Jesus if he approached them as he did Zaccheus?
3. Look at Zaccheus' actions in v. 6. How can these clues help us to understand him more deeply?
4. Some time passed between v. 7 and v. 8. We don't know how long or what Jesus and Zaccheus said to each other. But there were definite results. What were these results? Why do you think Zaccheus changed after this visit with Jesus?

C. Jesus and his life mission, vv. 9-10

5. How does this story illustrate Jesus' true manhood?
6. How does it illustrate his life mission stated in v. 10?
7. How does it illustrate the personal ways by which he carried out this mission?

Practical Themes — Choose the appropriate one.

a) Note that Jesus knew where to find needy people who were either rejected, ignored or forgotten by others. Who are our forgotten or neglected neighbours? How can we help them?
b) If we ourselves were outcasts (which we all are to some extent), what would be our response to Jesus' expression of interest and friendship?
c) How can Jesus change your life direction and habits? Do you want him to?

5 Jesus Kneels to Love
John 13:1-20

Context: We now see Jesus with his closest disciples in a special atmosphere. "The hour" had come. The conflict with Jewish officialdom was moving to what they wanted from the beginning: the arrest and death of the young radical before he completely upset their powerful, privileged status quo. Again it was the Feast of the Passover, loved by all good Jews. It was to be the last one which Jesus would celebrate with his disciples, for it was the night before his death.

Notes on the Text

v. 1   *Passover* See Word List.
        Jesus knew Cf. also vv. 3, 11. He also knew his disciples had just been arguing who of them would be appointed to the highest cabinet posts in his coming government! See Lk. 22:21-23.
v. 2   *Judas* This disciple had long shown evil motives in following Jesus. "Iscariot" was a name associated with extreme nationalism.
v. 4   *girded himself with a towel* A sign of the house slave who usually washed the guests' feet which were dusty from the dirt roads.

Development of Study/Discussion Questions

A.   What Jesus knew, vv. 1-5, 11, 18

1.   What different things did Jesus know? How did this knowledge affect his attitude to his disciples? How did it influence his actions?

2. Imagine yourself as one of the disciples when Jesus arose, took off his outer garment and put on the slave's towel! What would be your reaction?

Why do you think none of them had taken the initiative to wash the others' feet? What impresses you most about Jesus here?

B. What Simon Peter didn't know, vv. 6-11

3. If you were Simon Peter, what thoughts would have flashed through your mind? What feelings would have flooded over you? Why don't you want Jesus to wash your feet? Then why do you ask him to give you a complete bath?

4. How did Jesus respond to Simon Peter's apparent embarrassment and confusion?

As you listen carefully to their dialogue, what insight into Jesus' character and heart do you gain?

C. What the feet-washing meant, vv. 12-20

5. Several reasons prompted Jesus to wash his disciples' feet. What was the obvious reason? What was the symbolic reason? What was still another reason?

6. What have you gained in deeper understanding of Jesus' ministry to people?

Practical Themes —Choose the appropriate one.

a) What radical concept of leadership did Jesus teach his disciples? How do modern ideas of leadership differ?

b) Discuss one or two practical examples from everyday life where Jesus' example should be followed.

c) What was the spiritual significance of Jesus' symbolic act of washing the disciples' feet for us today?

6 Jesus Dies
John 19:17-30

Context: One third of the historical records about Jesus Christ is devoted to the last week of his life. So central in the Christian faith are the death and resurrection of this man. Soon after the last supper Jesus went to Gethsemane to pray. There Judas, disappointed that Jesus was not the expected political Messiah, betrayed him to the chief priests. Upon his arrest the eleven other disciples fled. Then followed a sleepless night of several intensive cross-questionings, alternately by Jewish and Roman officials. Pilate could have saved the innocent Jesus, but eventually handed him over to the bloodthirsty Jewish leaders.

Notes on the Text

v. 1   *Pilate* The Roman governor, who despised the Jews but could play politics with them.

v. 6   *Crucify him!* See 18:31 also. Crucifixion was the Roman method of execution, while stoning was the Jewish means. The OT, as well as Jesus himself, had predicted the Messiah would die by that means.

v. 9   *praetorium* Official residence of the Roman provincial governor.

v. 12   The Jews quickly switched the charge from blasphemy, a Jewish religious matter (v. 7), to treason, a Roman political matter.

v. 14   *sixth hour* Noon by Jewish reckoning.

v. 26   *the disciple whom he loved:* The author John, who was the youngest disciple, perhaps less than 20 at that time.

Development of Study/Discussion Questions

A.   Hate and indifference, vv. 17-24

1.   How do modern means of capital punishment compare
     with crucifixion?   Yet how do most people today re-
     gard the symbol of the cross?   Why?
2.   The historical cross of Jesus was anything but sentimen-
     tal. Consider people's feelings about it that day Jesus
     was crucified. What do you think the cross represented
     to Pilate?   to the chief priests?   to the soldiers?
     How can religious leaders like the priests become so
     hard?

B.   Love from the cross, vv. 25-27

3.   In contrast, no other biblical picture is more beautiful
     than the one drawn by Jesus' last words to his mother
     and a disciple in vv. 25-27. How much can we know
     about that disciple from this passage?   about Mary?
4.   What was Jesus' personal concern for his mother and for
     John?   What could make a man, agonising in a slow,
     torturous death, be so selfless?

C.   "It is finished", vv. 28-30

5.   Note the physically human side of Jesus. The vinegar
     probably gave him the final energy for his last cry.
     What, according to Jesus, was finished?
6.   "Jesus dies" might suggest that like other men's death,
     his was inevitable and beyond control. But compare v.
     30b with John 10:14-18. Who ultimately controlled
     Jesus' death?

Reflection: Why did Jesus die?   Ponder this great historical
act of Jesus' death for us and its meaning — the only possible
means of salvation. What can be the only reasonable response
of a thoughtful person?

7 Jesus Rises from Death
John 20:1-31

Context: "If Christ has not been raised, your faith is futile, and you are still in your sins" (I Cor. 15:17). Christianity holds together or falls apart, depending on whether or not Christ did indeed rise from death. This is why men seeking to destroy Christianity have usually first attacked the historicity of Jesus' resurrection.

Three sceptics who tried this carefully investigated the evidences. In the end they were converted to Jesus Christ! Sir Gilbert West went on to write *Observations on the History and Evidences of the Resurrection of Jesus Christ*. Gen. Lew Wallace eventually produced the influential Christian novel, *Ben-Hur*, which was also made into a film. And the lawyer Frank Morison was finally compelled to write *Who Moved the Stone?*, one of the most readable books on the subject.

Indeed so vital is this subject and our personal understanding of it, that we will spend two sessions on it. (Note Part 1 and Part 2) The author selected four of Jesus' followers and the disciples as a group to show how differently they came to believe that he had indeed returned from death. Observe the uniqueness of each situation.

Notes on the Text

v. 1   *Mary* The one from Magdala from whom Jesus had cast out seven demons and who thereafter served him faithfully (Lk. 8:1-2).

v. 2   *the other disciple* The author himself, the disciple John. See note on John 19:25 in preceding study.

v. 5   *linen cloths* The grave clothes made of many long lengths which were inter-leaved with embalming spices and wrapped tightly around the body like a mummy.

v. 15   *Woman* See Word List.

v. 23   As God had sent Jesus to reconcile men to himself, so Jesus sent his disciples to continue this ministry in his authority.

Part 1)   John 20:1-18

Development of Study/Discussion Questions

A.   The first one there, vv. 1-3, 11-18

1.   As you read this section about Mary, note the details. How do they reveal her faith in Jesus? What kind of Jesus was she apparently thinking of when she visited the tomb?

2.   What did she conclude about the empty tomb? What do you think about Jesus in the way he approached her in this state? What deeper things about himself did he teach her?

B.   The next two there, vv. 2-10

3.   Now let's take a look at Simon Peter and John. As you watch them running to the tomb, what do you think they were expecting?

4.   When they saw the tomb empty (except for the grave clothes), how did each respond? How would you have responded to the empty tomb?
     What personal factors can make a man or woman respond differently to Jesus Christ in the face of the same solid evidences of his resurrection?

Reflection

What evidences for Jesus' resurrection do we have that the early disciples did not have? What practical implications for daily living can his resurrection have for people today?

81

Development of Study/Discussion Questions

A.   The ten behind locked doors, vv. 19-23

1.   And what about the disciples as a group?   Evidently the testimony of Mary, Simon Peter and John about the empty tomb increased rather than dissolved their fears! Could there be other reasons for locking themselves in?
2.   Suddenly the resurrected Jesus came to them! What words could you use to describe his attitude to them in this atmosphere?
3.   They had not fully believed him. Yet how did he show he fully trusted them?   (Imagine how stunned they must have been!)

B.   The last one there, vv. 24-29

4.   What seemed to be behind Thomas' doubt?   Can you feel sympathetic for him?
5.   Now watch the special attention Jesus gave to him a week later. Jesus was also sympathetic, but he went beyond sympathy to teach Thomas (and us) about real faith in himself. What are these lessons?
6.   Considering his recent doubts, how do you think Thomas could make such a full-blown confession of faith in Jesus?

Practical Themes — Choose the appropriate one.

a)   How encouraging it is for us to know that Jesus' closest disciples had problems in believing his greatest claim! How can this study help others who, like Thomas, believe but need help in their unbelief?
b)   Consider the author's last two verses (vv. 30-31) in this chapter. What has been his aim in recording for us the life, death and resurrection of Jesus Christ?

A Final Word

Why Did He Come?— Why Did He Die?

He was despised and rejected by men; a man of sorrows and acquainted with grief; and as one from whom men hide their faces he was despised, and we esteemed him not. Surely he has borne our griefs and carried our sorrows; yet we esteemed him stricken, smitten by God, and afflicted. But he was wounded for our transgressions, he was bruised for our iniquities; upon him was the chastisement that made us whole, and with his stripes we are healed. All we like sheep have gone astray; we have turned every one to his own way; and the Lord has laid on him the iniquity of us all. He was oppressed, and he was afflicted, yet he opened not his mouth; like a lamb that is led to the slaughter, and like a sheep that before its shearers is dumb, so he opened not his mouth. *Isaiah 53:3-7*

1. It might be worth our while to think why and when people hide their faces from someone else (v. 3). How do you think this applies to Jesus Christ?
2. How would you describe our "griefs" and "sorrows"? What, according to this passage, has caused them?
3. Compare Isaiah's prophecy with a passage from Peter's first letter:

   He committed no sin; no guile was found on his lips. When he was reviled, he did not revile in return; when he suffered, he did not threaten; but he trusted to him who judges justly. He himself bore our sins in his body on the tree, that we might die to sin and live to righteousness. By his wounds you have been healed. For you were straying like sheep, but have now returned to the Shepherd and Guardian of your souls. *I Peter 2:22-25*

It is alien to our common-sense thinking that another person should take upon his shoulders the consequences of our mistakes. Alien, perhaps. But is it not also necessary? And then: by his stripes and wounds we are healed: the dialectics of the Bible. How can we understand this?

E Learning to Know God

If you had known me, you would have known my Father also; henceforth you know him and have seen him.

John 14:7

The problem of God's existence and activity is as vital as ever in our materialistic society. Many people still have some kind of belief in God — but as an abstract force which is unknowable or as a kind of last resort for people in special need.

Jesus Christ was a teacher who claimed to be the Son of God and who taught that men could know God personally and not simply in an abstract, conceptual sense. He often used metaphors and parables which showed clearly the way to a vital knowledge of the God who created the universe, who created men as human beings, endowed with freedom and responsibility, destined to love and to be loved. Jesus is like a window, and through the window we can see the beautiful landscape of God's kingdom, and even God himself as the Heavenly Light.

1 As a Son Knows His Father
Luke 15:11-32

Context: The scribes and Pharisees considered themselves God's most faithful and strictest followers. Therefore, they objected to Jesus, whom they considered unorthodox. The present parable is the main part of his answer to their criticism that he liked to spend time with sinners (15:1-2).

Textual Notes

v. 12   *his share of the property*   A third part for a younger son (Dt. 21:17), obtained usually at the father's death; so this case was very unusual.

v. 15   *feed swine*   A very lowly work, for swine were unclean to Jews.

v. 18   *against heaven*   A Jewish substitute for using God's name directly.

v. 19   *hired servants*   A social status lower than that of a slave, since they could be dismissed by their master anytime he wished.

v. 22   The *best robe* was a mark of honour; the *ring* was a mark of authority; *shoes* were worn only by freemen, not slaves.

Development of Study/Discussion Questions

A.   The younger son, vv. 11-21

1.   As you watch this young man, what do you find attractive about him? Why do you suppose he leaves home? What things happen to disillusion him?

2.   At what point does a change begin in his life? What memories and hopes bring this about? Note which word is repeated in vv. 17-19. What does this reveal about the original relationship of the father and son?

B. **The father and the younger son, vv. 11-12, 22-24**

3. In the first part of this parable Jesus says little about the
    father. Yet what kind of fatherly traits can you see even
    here (vv. 11-12)?
4. Observe the details Jesus describes in the reunion. How
    do they reveal the father's deeper traits?   (vv. 20-24)

C. **The elder son, vv. 25-28**

5. In what details does Jesus draw the character of the
    elder son?   As a result, what kind of person do you
    see?
    Have you ever known such people?   What made them
    like that?

D. **The father and the elder son, vv. 28-32**

6. What important quality of the father does Jesus convey
    by the statement, "His father came out and entreated
    him"?
7. What is the elder son's image of himself?   How does it
    also reveal his evaluation of a) his father?   b) their
    relationship?   How does v. 30 reveal his relationship to
    his brother?
8. In response, how does the father correct the elder son's
    wrong thinking?   Even in correction, what is still his
    attitude to this son?

Themes for Reflection — Choose the applicable one for discussion.

a) From the way that Jesus tells this story, what does he
    want us to know about God?   about ourselves?   about
    the basis of true, lasting happiness?   Why do you think
    he ends his story without saying what was the elder
    son's final response?
b) What is your basic understanding of God?   What are
    your reasons for thinking of him in this way?
c) In what way do you prodigalise?   In what way does
    mankind prodigalise?   Do you share the younger son's
    disillusion with life?

2 As a Sheep Knows His Shepherd
John 10:1-18

Context: Jesus had just opened the eyes of a man born blind. Despite the Pharisees' warning not to do so, the man openly acknowledged that Jesus had healed him. Consequently they "cast him out" (i.e., barred him from the assembly of the synagogue). Jesus' teaching in this present chapter directly challenged these false religious teachers/leaders of the people.

Textual Notes

v. 1   *sheepfold* An enclosure for the sheep to rest having only one door.

v. 3   *name* See Word List.

sheep Different sheep belonging to different shepherds slept together. In the morning each sheep knew instinctively to which shepherd he belonged.

v. 4   *know* In biblical language "to know" is not merely knowing with one's mind, but with a fuller, more intimate and encompassing knowledge.

v. 7   *door* The shepherd himself slept across the entrance.

v. 12   *hireling* Someone paid to work temporarily.

v. 16   *other sheep. . .one flock* Gentiles uniting with Jews.

Development of Study/Discussion Questions

A.   Thieves, robbers and strangers, vv. 1-10

1.   It is interesting that Jesus does not call the religious leaders false shepherds, but something worse. Why?

2.   List what Jesus says about the thieves, robbers and strangers. What is always their aim?   How does Jesus' aim differ?
Why do you think he uses this indirect attack on the Pharisees and scribes?

B. The shepherd who knows his sheep, vv. 1-10

3. How else does Jesus contrast himself with the thieves and robbers?
4. What does he know about his sheep? Which of their characteristics does he stress? In what different ways does he say he cares for them?
5. These are all very bold claims! What can make a man dare to talk like this before the hostile religious leaders? How would you feel with such a leader?

C. The good shepherd who dies for the sheep, vv.11-18

6. Again Jesus teaches more about himself by contrast with another kind of person. How is the hireling different from the shepherd? What makes the differences in their attitudes to the safety and security of the sheep? Who might these hirelings be?
7. How would you describe Jesus' relationship to God by what he says here?
   What is the connection between "loving" and "laying down one's life"?
8. What different things does he say about his death? What are your impressions about a man who talks about his death and resurrection like this?
9. From this extended picture of the good shepherd and his sheep, summarise a) Jesus' relationship to those who follow him; b) the results of following him; c) Jesus' main mission on earth.

Themes for Reflection —Choose the applicable one for discussion.

a) Jesus made it clear that he chose to die. But people then did not understand this. Do you know why Jesus died voluntarily for us?
b) What must we do to enter into the sheepfold? What are the implications of Jesus' saying "I am the door"?

3 As a Subject Knows His King
Matthew 22:1-14

Context: Most of Jesus' parables against the hypocrisy and other sins of the contemporary religious leaders were told to them in Jerusalem during the last week of his life. He knew they would soon kill him. Yet he missed no opportunity to teach about the kingdom of God and his listeners' responsibility to the King.

Textual Notes

v. 1 *parable* See Word List.
v. 2 *kingdom of heaven:* See Word List.
      marriage feast A prominent community event lasting several days. In a culture not run by clocks or calendar, the first invitation went out early and was followed by a second or third invitation when the day drew near.
vv. 3-7 Jesus may be historically referring to Israel (God's people) in the OT, or prophetically to the fall of Jerusalem in AD 70.
v. 13 *outer darkness* See Word List.

Development of Study/Discussion Questions

A. Jesus' use of parables, v. 1

1. Jesus often used parables. In what ways are they effective?

B. The king's invitations to the elite, vv. 2-7

2. What important comparisons is Jesus suggesting in v. 2?
3. How would you feel if you were invited to a royal wedding celebration? It seems strange that the twice

invited guests do not respond positively. What do their negative responses tell us about their opinion of their king?

4. Do you think the king is just in his reaction to the guests' ungrateful behaviour? What are your reasons for this view?

C. The king's invitations to the public, vv. 8-10

5. Why does the king issue more invitations? What does this tell us about him?
    This time what kind of people does he command his servants to invite? What do you suppose Jesus means by the "bad and good"?

D. A man without the wedding garment, vv. 11-14

6. Guests always wore special garments for the great occasion, provided by the host or themselves. What then does the man without one reveal about his regard for the host king? (See also v. 14)
    What is Jesus suggesting to his Pharisee listeners through the king's question and the man's response in v. 12?

7. As in v. 7, the punishment in v. 13 seems extremely harsh. What does Jesus intend his listeners to understand through this about God and his ways? How does he intend v. 14 to sharpen this understanding?

8. *Conclusion:* Through this parable what characteristics of God does Jesus want us to see? What kind of people will be found in God's kingdom?

Themes for Reflection —Choose the applicable one for discussion.

a) In what way does the Eternal King invite us today?
b) What is the meaning of the wedding garment? What are the prerequisites for receiving it?

91

4 As a Servant Knows His Master
Matthew 25:14-30

Context: Jesus told this parable to his disciples in the same week as the last one we studied — a few days before his death. For his enemies were climaxing their deadly opposition to this young peasant rabbi. This parable is part of the final, intensive training of his twelve disciples, the men to whom he was committing the task of carrying on his work.

Textual Notes

Do not confuse this parable with Luke 19:11-27, which has many similarities, but also many differences.

v. 15   *talent* See Word List.
v. 18   *in the ground* Considered then as minimum requirement for safety.
v. 24   These were proverbs about making gain by other people's efforts.
v. 30   *outer darkness* See Word List.

Development of Study/Discussion Questions

A.   The master's commitments, vv. 14-18

1.   The story is uncomplicated in details. But behind the first simple facts in vv. 14-15, what can you learn about the main character?

2. Observe the contrast between the first two servants and the third servant. What different attitudes to their master can you see by what they do with their master's money?
   What do you think Jesus intends the talents to represent?

B. The master's commendations, vv. 19-23

3. What might Jesus be indicating to his disciples by the "long time" before the master returns?
4. With what is the master most pleased in the first two servants?
   What could Jesus possibly mean by his reward for them — "Enter into the joy of your master"?

C. The master's condemnation, vv. 24-30

5. Examine the third servant's excuse for not investing his master's money. What picture of his master has he? How accurate is it?
6. The servant says his motive was fear of the master, but how does his master disagree with him?
7. Does Jesus' principle of "take and give" in vv. 28-29 make sense to you? In what ways?
8. *Conclusion:* What is the central meaning of the whole parable? If it is not "to make money", then what is it? Is Jesus preaching capitalism?!?

Themes for Reflection — Choose the applicable one for discussion.

a) Do you have any concept of God as someone to whom you are responsible?
b) How are you using your abilities and resources, and fulfilling the assignments which God has given to you? What are your criteria for discerning and investing them and acting in the right way?
c) Would you some day like to hear God say to you, "Well done, good and faithful servant. Enter into the joy of your master"? What can make this possible?

5 As a Man Knows His Friend
John 15:9-17

Context: This intimate conversation is part of Jesus' last moving meeting with the men closest to himself on the night before his death. Jesus tells them two momentous facts — that one of them would betray him and that the Holy Spirit would come as his substitute (Ch. 13-14). Then he discusses the conditions for and characteristics of the deeper relationship he would have with them (15:1-8).

Textual Notes

v. 9   *love agape* (Gk), the highest form of love, which wants the best for the other person, regardless of his condition or attitude.

v. 15   *servants* "Slaves", who belong to their master without any rights.

v. 16   *fruit* Natural, expected result of a healthy organism.
my name Equivalent to "my authority" or "my personal guarantee".

Development of Study/Discussion Questions

A.   The pattern of love, vv. 9-12

1.   Jesus now describes the love that characterises his relationship with the disciples. What examples of love relationships does he set forth?

2.   Note Jesus' repeated commandment for his disciples to love one another. (Cf. 13:34-35, 15:12, 17) What does this imply about their relationship then?   If Jesus *commands* them to love, then what part of man is he appealing to — emotions, mind or will?   Have you experienced this kind of love?

3. Note how different from the world's concept of love is Jesus' concept. He shows that love implies both freedom and obligation. How can these two concepts of being free and keeping his commandments be reconciled?

B. Characteristics of true friends, vv. 13-15

4. According to Jesus what is the greatest way of showing love for a friend? What is he indicating about himself in this same verse? In what possible ways could a person today "lay down his life for his friends", apart from dying?

5. What is the basic condition for being a friend of Jesus Christ? Compare vv. 10, 12, 17. Do you think it is possible to be good friends without loyalty and obedience? Please explain.

6. What does Jesus imply by saying "no longer" in v. 15? What does he say is the basic difference between a servant and a friend? In what sense had the disciples been "servants" to Jesus?

C. Friends who are fruitful, vv. 16-17

7. Which other unique characteristics does Jesus discuss about friendship with himself?

8. What could be the fruit that Jesus expects from his disciple-friends? How is it possible, according to Jesus, to bear this kind of fruit?
As you review this passage, what to you is the most striking truth that Jesus is teaching about friendship with him?

Themes for Reflection — Choose the applicable one for discussion.

a) Does your friendship with God bear fruit in loving others? How can you learn to bear more fruit that is lasting?

b) This kind of human/divine friendship is still possible. If you are not yet sure you are a friend of Jesus Christ, see Revelation 3:20 for how you can begin this friendship.

6

Context: After a tiring day of teaching the crowds, Jesus and his twelve disciples had crossed the lake to get some rest. A storm suddenly arose. Jesus calmed it with his command, and his authority over nature awed them. When they landed, another crisis awaited them.

Textual Notes

v. 26   *Gerasenes*   A tract of land bordering Lake Galilee, evidently controlled by Gerasa, a city about 40 miles SE of the lake.

v. 27   *demons*   Also referred to as "devils" or "evil spirits"; invisible personal beings who are subject to Satan.

v. 30   *Legion*   Latin word meaning a great number of people, like an army capable of oppressing another nation by their strength. Here it means many evil forces dividing the man's personality.

v. 31   *abyss*   A prison for disobedient spirits; "bottomless pit" in Revelation 20:1-3.

v. 32   *swine*   Unclean animals for Jews, who were not allowed even to touch them. The herdsmen were probably Gentiles or unorthodox Jews.

Development of Study/Discussion Questions

A.   Reality of Satan's power, vv. 26-29

1.   Nowhere else in the Bible is a demoniac described more vividly than here. What details does Luke give about him? What effects do the demons have on the man?

2. What attitude do they express toward Jesus? What do they know about him?
    In what ways does this demon-filled man symbolise the human condition in general?

B. **Reality of Jesus' power, vv. 30-33**

3. Trace step by step how Jesus deals with the situation. What is significant about each step? What do Jesus' actions reveal about himself?
4. Some people have criticised Jesus for upsetting the local economy! How would you answer this charge from Jesus' viewpoint?

C. **Clear-cut responses to Jesus, vv. 34-39**

5. Recall how Luke (a doctor) vividly described the demoniac before he met Jesus. How does he now describe the change in him?
6. What are the varied reactions of the people when they see the healed man? Why?
7. How is the healed man's response different from the people's? Can you suggest reasons why Jesus does not allow him to follow him back to Galilee?

Themes for Reflection — Choose the applicable one for discussion.

a) Consider Jesus' last instructions to the man. What can we learn about discipleship under Jesus' lordship from this?
b) Why have people become so interested in the occults? What relevance does this passage have to this interest?
c) What powers dominate present-day life, and your own life in particular? How do they affect your personality? How far do you believe that an encounter with Jesus can make changes in people?

7

God's Power & Human Finiteness
Luke 8:40-42, 49-56

Context: News of Jesus' healing the demoniac and the subsequent events (see preceding study) had evidently run ahead of his return to the opposite side of Lake Galilee. Among the eager crowd were individuals with extreme human need, challenging Jesus and his disciples with equally dramatic tensions.

Textual Notes

v. 41   *a ruler of the synagogue*   An elder who arranged synagogue services and other community affairs.

v. 50   Cf. Jn. 11:25-26.

v. 51   *Peter, James, John*   The inner circle of the Twelve. Cf. 9:28 and Mk. 14:33.

v. 52   *weeping and bewailing*   In the ancient East funeral rites took place immediately after death and included professional mourners.

Development of Study/Discussion Questions

A.   The crowd and Jesus, vv. 40-42

1.   What does the crowd see in Jesus that attracts them? How different do you think their interest is from that of Jairus the respected community leader?
     What facts can we gather about Jairus in vv. 41-42? How can our personal circumstances affect our attitude to Jesus?

B.   Jairus and Jesus, vv. 49-51

2.   Jesus' healing of the woman with hemorrhage is a study in itself. It is enough to note here that this "interrup-

tion" must greatly test Jairus' faith. What else probably tests Jairus' faith in Jesus?

3. Note that v. 50 says Jesus answered Jairus, though there has been no question. For what does Jesus know about his reaction to the message?

Consider the contrast between fear and faith. What does Jesus teach us here about the relationship between the two?

In what way then does Jesus proceed to strengthen Jairus' faith? How can he have confidence in such circumstances?

C. The mourners and Jesus, vv. 52-53

4. What can be some reasons that Jesus takes only Peter, James, John and the parents into the house?

5. Contrast Jesus and the mourners. Why do you think Luke specifically includes v. 53? What does Jesus mean by "She is not dead but asleep"?

D. The parents and Jesus, vv. 54-56

6. In vv. 54-55 what interesting details about Jesus' raising the girl from death do you observe? What do they tell you of his character?

7. Why do you think Jesus forbids the parents to tell anyone about what has happened? What circumstances make these instructions of Jesus different from those to the demoniac in the previous study?

Themes for Reflection — Choose the applicable one for discussion.

a) As you trace the progress of Jairus' faith in Jesus, at which step do you find your own faith?

b) Discuss various attitudes to death, including the Christian one.

c) Consider the implications of Jesus' authority over "death, man's last enemy". What do they tell us about Jesus' essential identity?

A Final Word

The fear of the Lord is the beginning of wisdom.

Praise the Lord!
I will give thanks to the Lord with my whole heart,
    in the company of the upright, in the congregation.
Great are the works of the Lord,
    studied by all who have pleasure in them.
Full of honour and majesty is his work,
    and his righteousness endures for ever.
He has caused his wonderful works to be remembered;
    the Lord is gracious and merciful.
He provides food for those who fear him;
    he is ever mindful of his covenant.
He has shown his people the power of his works,
    in giving them the heritage of the nations.
The works of his hands are faithful and just;
    all his precepts are trustworthy.
They are established for ever and ever,
    to be performed with faithfulness and uprightness.
He sent redemption to his people,
    he has commanded his covenant for ever.
    Holy and terrible is his name!
The fear of the Lord is the beginning of wisdom;
    a good understanding have all those who practise it.
His praise endures for ever! *Psalm 111*

F Jesus the Compassionate One

Nearly all people, whether they believe in God or not, like the idea of God as a God of love. It is not offensive. Ours is a world hungry for a love that is fulfilling. Thus many people conclude God's love surely must be the highest level of all love. Yet it remains a warm but abstract idea, desired but not personally grasped.

We want to introduce Jesus of Nazareth to you. Many believe he is the Son of God. If He is, then he must exhibit the abstract idea of God's love in the concrete — the real, the observable — for all to see. The selected passages, from the historical records of the New Testament Gospels, demonstrate many characteristics of Jesus, but we have focused on his compassion.

Whether or not one has compassion in many different situations is the test of fire. This test clearly shows if one has this highest level of love for others. It costs something to be compassionate. Compassion cannot be expressed in a vacuum, nor can it be shown only at one's own convenience. That would be "charity", not compassion.

It is the aim of these studies that you may see Jesus as he really is: "The Compassionate One", whose love survived all the fiery tests of love for his fellow men. May you respond to him through these studies, not in the abstract, but in personal reality, as he responded in compassion for you in time and space — history.

1   Does God Really Care?
John 11:1-44

Introduction: Have a short discussion about the difficulties we feel when there seems to be no solution and we ask, Does God really care at all about my case? This was how two good friends of Jesus felt in a similar situation.

Notes on the Text

vv. 1-2   See John 12:1-8 and also Luke 10:38-42.
v. 4   See also Mk. 5:35-39 for Jesus' view of death.
v. 7   *Judea*   The center of official opposition to Jesus.
v. 8   *Jews*   See Word List.
v. 17   *four days*   The custom was immediate burial.
vv. 33-38   Not only sorrow for Lazarus and his sisters made Jesus weep, but facing death, the worst that sin brings.

Questions for Study and Discussion

A.   Problems for everyone! vv. 1-16

1.   Obviously Lazarus' illness is dangerous, or Mary and Martha would not send for Jesus. What do they expect Jesus to do about their problem?
2.   As you listen to the dialogue in vv. 7-16, what do you see as a) the disciples' great concern? b) Jesus' great concern?
3.   What might be the feelings of the sisters when Jesus does not come on time? Why does he let them suffer?

B.   Martha and Mary, vv. 17-37

4.   Observe Martha and Mary in the way they approach Jesus. What similarities and differences do you see?
5.   What do these verses reveal about Mary's and Martha's attitudes toward Lazarus and the possibility of his return to life? What does v. 39 make clear?

C. Jesus, the Resurrection and the Life, vv. 1-44

6. Note the background of this story: hostility towards Jesus in Judea, Thomas' fatalistic words in v. 16, Jesus' approaching death. Yet he dares to go to Bethany, and he dares to raise a man from the dead.
   What does Jesus mean by his words in v. 9? Look carefully at the way he uses the words "day" and "walking in the day without stumbling". What can we learn from this verse about trusting God?
7. Each of Jesus' miracles not only has an intrinsic value, but it forms part of God's total revelation of himself to mankind. What are the different symbolic values of this story? What can we learn about the fulfilment of God's promises to man now and in the future? (See vv. 25-26 in particular)

D. God cares enough to weep

8. Observe Jesus' responses to people and their problems. What is his response a) to intellectual reasonings in times of difficulty (vv. 21-26), and b) to emotional experiences under stress (vv. 33-37)?
9. Jesus does not meet the problem of Mary and Martha in the way they expect. But what do his actions ultimately show about his view of suffering?
   In what new light do Mary and Martha see their family friend because of the suffering he let them go through?

Questions for Application — Choose one for discussion.

a) What do you learn from Jesus about how to respond to human crisis?
b) Take another close look at vv. 25-26. Now try to express the meaning of "living" in the light of Jesus' teaching here.
c) What kind of faith in Jesus does the sisters' problem demand of them? How would your faith compare in a similar situation?

2 The Compassionate Creator
Mark 6:30-44

Introduction: One thing that man needs and desires is rest. The Bible speaks of the responsibility of work; it also recommends the delight of rest. However, sometimes even well-deserved rest has to be postponed for service. It is a special kind of love that enables a person to forfeit his rights in order to meet the needs of others. This quality of love is the subject of our passage.

Notes on the Text

v. 31   *lonely place*   Uninhabited region east of Lake Galilee.

v. 33   *ahead of them*   Going eastward their boat evidently met the strong easterly winds that made them slower than the crowd on foot.

v. 34   *sheep. . .shepherd*   A common OT analogy of God and his people, the sheep being of all domestic animals most prone to stray.

v. 44   *five thousand men*   Mt. 14:21 adds "besides women and children".

Questions for Study and Discussion

A.   Sensitivity to the disciples' needs, vv. 30-32

1.   Earlier in this chapter (vv. 7-13), Jesus sent out his twelve disciples for the first time on a mission without him. And now they have returned. How does v. 30 indicate what their report to Jesus is probably like?

2.   Why does Jesus want them to withdraw to a lonely place?

B. Sensitivity to the crowd's needs, vv. 33-38

3. Imagine how the tired disciples must feel when they are greeted by the crowd! What can we know about these people from vv. 33-34? What do they apparently want from Jesus?
4. How does Jesus immediately respond to the crowd? Why? How does the disciples' attitude to the crowd differ from Jesus'? Do they have a right to feel this way? What's your reason for thinking so?
When the impossible is demanded of us, what is our usual reaction, especially when we're tired and hungry?
5. What does Jesus see as the crowd's *immediate* need? What does he see as a *deeper* need?
6. Reflecting on Jesus' example here, what characteristics of real compassion do you see?

C. Sensitivity to the disciples' training, vv. 39-44

7. In this part of the event Jesus is accomplishing two purposes at once — to feed the crowd and to teach his disciples some deeper lessons. What are these lessons for the men who are to carry on his work?

Questions for Application — Choose one for discussion.

a) In what ways are we like the disciples in this story? What can we learn from them about working for and with Jesus Christ?
b) To what extent do the needs of the crowd reflect our needs today? Discuss concrete situations.
This is the only miracle recorded in all four Gospels — a clear example of Jesus' power to meet the needs of humanity, although not perhaps in the way we would expect (e.g., efficiently applying rational techniques like planning, organisation or technology). How is Jesus Christ able to meet the needs of our day? What can we learn about his power to use the small and seemingly insignificant things of life?

3   A Blind Man Sees the King
Mark 10:46-52

Introduction: The fame of Jesus of Nazareth had spread widely. One can imagine that the stories and rumours of his miracles, teaching and healings were common topics of conversation. The crowds grew. Yet one can see that in the midst of any crowd, Jesus still cared for the individual. In this passage he was nearing Jerusalem and certain death by his enemies. Let's see what happens.

Notes on the Text

v. 46   *Jericho* See Word List.
        Bartimaeus Literally "the son of filth".
v. 47   *Jesus of Nazareth* See "Nazareth" in Word List.
        Son of David See Word List.

Questions for Study and Discussion

A.   The Son of Filth, vv. 46-48

1.   It is unusual that a "nobody" like a blind beggar would be identified by a name. What else does Mark tell us about Bartimaeus?   Can you imagine having a name like that — "son of filth"! How would such a person feel about himself?
2.   From hints in the text what can we know about the crowd?   What is their attitude to Bartimaeus?   How does their attitude to Jesus differ from Bartimaeus' attitude to Jesus?
3.   What does Bartimaeus' reaction to the crowd tell us about him?   Note his repetitious call to the "Son of David". What does this imply about his faith in Jesus of Nazareth?

B.   The Son of David, vv. 49-50

4.   Try to visualise and feel the drama here. Jesus and the crowd are nearing Jerusalem. He hears someone shouting that rare Messianic title, "Son of David". How do you think he reacts?
5.   Note the details of Bartimaeus' response to Jesus' call to him. The whole Bible is God's personal call to man. Why do people not respond as eagerly as Bartimaeus?

C.   The King's crucial question, vv. 51-52

6.   Why does Jesus ask Bartimaeus this particular question in v. 51?   Can he not tell what a blind beggar wants? Explain.
7.   Look at Bartimaeus' answer carefully. What more does it tell us about him?
8.   When you look at all Jesus' statements together (vv. 49, 51, 52), what do you discover about his way of building up Bartimaeus' faith?
      In what special ways is Jesus' healing Bartimaeus an act of compassion?

Questions for Application — Choose one for discussion.

a)   What can we follow in Bartimaeus' example of faith and hope in Jesus Christ?
b)   Like the other Gospel writers Mark records events in a certain order. As in the previous study, this event takes place just before Jesus' death. Think of the growing enmity of the Jews, their unwillingness to see Jesus as their true Messiah. We must ask ourselves again what the symbolic meaning of this miracle is. What is he telling us in placing this story just before Jesus' entry into Jerusalem?   What strikes you most in Jesus' behaviour in this awkward period of his life?

4 Nearness Doesn't Make Neighbourliness
Luke 10:25-37

Introduction: Jews and Samaritans had had hundreds of years of mutual animosity. Jews despised Samaritans as an impure race with a false religion, worshiping God on Mt. Gerizim instead of in Jerusalem. In 445 B.C. they had opposed and mocked the Jews who were rebuilding the walls of Jerusalem after exile. More recently, between A.D. 6 to 9, they had desecrated the Temple during the Passover Feast by scattering animal bones on the floor.

Notes on the Text

v. 25   *lawyer*   An expert in the Jewish law (first five books of the OT).
          eternal life   See Word List.
v. 30   *going down to Jericho*   See Word List.
v. 31   *priest*   Those who performed the temple sacrifices and ceremonies.
v. 32   *Levite*   Those who assisted the priests and interpreted the law.
v. 35   *denarii*   See Word List.

Questions for Study and Discussion

A.   A lawyer tests Jesus, vv. 25-29

1.   Insincere people can ask basic religious questions and give correct biblical answers. What is the lawyer's motive in questioning Jesus?
2.   What do you think is Jesus' intention in answering with another question? How correct is the lawyer's reply? See Dt. 6:5 and Lv. 19:8.

3. How does the lawyer's second question further reveal his motive? Why does he think he can "justify himself" with this question?

B. Jesus answers the test, vv. 30-35

4. Again Jesus refuses to be trapped by the lawyer's next question. He answers with a parable. How is a well-told story powerful in communicating truth?
5. Why do you think Jesus uses the priest and Levite in this story? What may be reasons that both of them bypass the victim?
6. What does it cost the Samaritan to get involved with the victim? Why do you think Jesus chooses a Samaritan as the example of compassion?
   According to Jesus' story how do you define a compassionate neighbour?
7. What does Jesus' story tell us about the way he looks at the law as interpreted by the religious establishment?

C. Jesus tests the lawyer, vv. 36-37

8. Jesus asks the lawyer to draw his own conclusions. How does he change his question about the neighbour? Why?
   Jesus knows the lawyer is clever and has "all the right answers". So what is his challenge to him twice? (v. 28 and v. 37)
   In summary, what is Jesus' answer to the lawyer's two questions?

Questions for Application — Choose one for discussion.

a) What contact points with your life do you find in this passage?
b) What are the implications for us in Jesus' change of question from "Who is my neighbour?" to "Who proves to be neighbour to me?"
c) Think of a person in your daily contacts whose social class you dislike. How could you show compassion to him or her?

5 From Terror to Freedom
John 8:1-11

Introduction: John's Gospel presents Jesus Christ, God himself become man, in a series of confrontations with the opposing religious leaders of his day. They were constantly trying to trap him in order to have a pretext for arresting and destroying him. In Ch. 7 the religious leaders had failed in an attempt to arrest Jesus, for one of their number, sympathetic with Jesus, had pointed out that they had no real charge against him.

Notes on the Text

v. 3   *scribes, Pharisees* See Word List.
v. 5   *Moses and the law* See Word List. See also Lv. 20:10 for their deliberate misinterpretation of its application of the punishment for adultery.
v. 6   *stooped down* A recognised sign of unwillingness to listen. Cf. v. 8.

Questions for Study and Discussion

A.   The Pharisees' fail-proof trap, vv. 1-6

1.   The scribes and Pharisees are sure this time they can trap Jesus. What are the only answers they think Jesus can have to their question? How do they hope to corner Jesus in each case?

B.   The woman caught in the act, vv. 3-5

2.   Try to put yourself in the woman's place and describe her feelings in each succeeding verse as the narrative progresses. How would you feel standing before Jesus if the most shameful thing in your life has suddenly been made public? Would you stay or run?

3.   How is her self-respect, even apart from her adultery, destroyed?

C. Jesus' third option, vv. 6-11

4. Observe the steps by which Jesus directs his accusers' thoughts towards their own guilt. What do you see about his method? What does their reaction to Jesus' challenge tell us about what is happening within them?

5. Consider Jesus' dilemma before the crowd and their accusing leaders. Yet for whom is he concerned? Why? Recall how the scribes and Pharisees have destroyed whatever self-respect the woman has had. How does Jesus, in spite of her adultery, restore it?

6. This story seems to contradict all moral codes and to challenge the accepted law and order. It is one of the most radical of Jesus' deeds, with far-reaching consequences. Controversy about the authorship of this story and its place in John's Gospel reveals something of the hesitancy on the part of the established churches to include it in the canon of Scripture.
Is Jesus being too radical here? What does the essential truth of the story teach us about Jesus our Saviour?

D. Who judges and who forgives?

7. Compare this story with Ps. 130:3, 4 and Ro. 8:33, 34. How does it illustrate these passages?

Questions for Application — Choose one for discussion.

a) How can Jesus pronounce forgiveness on someone who clearly has broken God's law, and still claim to do only those things that please God? Does Jesus teach passivity or resignation towards injustice in the world and in our human relationships?

b) What can we learn about our own criticism and judgment of others? What is the relationship between judgment and grace as seen in Jesus Christ?

c) What would you do if you were one of the woman's accusers after you left the temple?

A Final Word

That he might rescue us from all our evil ways and make for Himself a people of His own, clean and pure, with our hearts set upon a life that is good. *Titus 2:14, (Philips)*

"For the grace of God has appeared for the salvation of all men, training us to renounce irreligion and worldly passions, and to live sober, upright, and godly lives in this world, awaiting our blessed hope, the appearing of the glory of our great God and Saviour Jesus Christ, who gave himself for us to redeem us from all iniquity and to purify for himself a people of his own who are zealous for good deeds.

"Declare these things; exhort and reprove with all authority. Let no one disregard you.

"Remind them to be submissive to rulers and authorities, to be obedient, to be ready for any honest work, to speak evil of no one, to avoid quarreling, to be gentle, and to show perfect courtesy toward all men. For we ourselves were once foolish, disobedient, led astray, slaves to various passions and pleasures, passing our days in malice and envy, hated by men and hating one another; but when the goodness and loving kindness of God our Saviour appeared, he saved us, not because of deeds done by us in righteousness, but in virtue of his own mercy, by the washing of regeneration and renewal in the Holy Spirit, which he poured out upon us richly through Jesus Christ our Saviour, so that we might be justified by his grace and become heirs in hope of eternal life. The saying is sure." *Titus 2:11 – 3:8*

"The grace of God teaches us". Thinking of the human situation as described in 3:3, we can imagine that a merciful God might forgive us. But that He can regenerate us, save us, pull us out of our hopeless situation, is more difficult to grasp. Yet, without this, the life and work of Jesus Christ would be meaningless.

Conversion *(metanoia)* must be understood very literally: turn away, turn around, allow God to pull you out. Why? So that we may be taught, by the grace of God, a different way to walk and to live, a life that is good, clean, righteous.

"What does it profit, my brethren, if a man says he has faith but has not works?. . .For as the body apart from the spirit is dead, so faith apart from works is dead." *James 2:14, 26*

G Jesus the Radical

According to Josephus, the second-century Jewish historian, Zealot guerilla warfare and revolts in Palestine broke out against Rome about once in a generation. Even among Jesus' twelve closest disciples, possibly five had Zealot connections. Throughout his ministry Jesus himself was pressured to use Zealot-like revolutionary methods to achieve his aim.

But Jesus was not a revolutionary. For a revolutionary is an "outsider" bent on sabotaging the whole existent structure. Indeed one can say that Jesus sought to maintain some of the forms and procedures of his society. He faithfully attended and supported the synagogue, the prevalent religious form of his day, and he loved the Temple for what it represented.

Nor was he a reformist, tearing pieces from new garments to mend a moth-eaten garment. He aimed for lasting results, not temporary effects.

Jesus was a radical. He was an "insider" who cared profoundly enough about people and human life to go to the root* of personal worthiness and meaningful social relationships. He came to radicalise the heart, that restless seat of human desires and ambitions.

---

*The word "radical" comes from the Latin radix, which means "root".

(The first three studies in this series, as well as the last two in "Jesus: Man and Saviour", are taken from Ada Lum, Jesus the Radical (FES: Malaysia and IVP: USA), and used by permission)

1 He Upsets the Capitalists
John 2:13-25

Introduction: This event is preceded by the first significant events of Jesus' public ministry in his province of Galilee in northern Palestine. He is 30 now. Here the scene is the capital of Jerusalem in the south during the Passover feast. It is Jesus' first public appearance.

Notes on the Text

v. 13   *Passover* See Word List.

v. 14   Selling sacrificial animals and exchanging money for the pilgrims began as a convenience. But it grew into business, controlled by the priests and Pharisees. Pharisees.

v. 15   *whip of cords* Not a weapon but a symbol of authority and judgment.

v. 18   *the Jews* See Word List.
      sign A divine seal of authority.

vv. 21-22 Neither Jesus' critics nor disciples understood this prediction of his resurrection. But it had "faith value" for sincere seekers. If those religious leaders had followed the truth they had, God would have led them to more truth, as He did the disciples.

Study/Discussion Questions

A.   Jesus' response to the temple commercialism, vv. 13-17

1.   How mixed Jesus' feelings must be —excited as a worshipper approaching the holy temple, then sad and angry, seeing all the commercialism! How does he respond?
Why is Jesus so passionate? How justified do you think his actions are?

2.   What is Jesus' attitude to the temple? (vv. 16-17) How does this contrast with the Jews' attitude?
We physical creatures need concrete symbols to remind us of spiritual realities. What was the purpose of the temple?

116

B.   The Jews' challenge to the peasant carpenter, vv. 18-21

3.   The radical action of a young peasant carpenter from the despised town of Nazareth is bound to bring out the wrath of the religious establishment. After all, what threat confronts them?   What is their basic question to Jesus?
     What do we learn about these religious leaders from their reactions to Jesus and his actions?
4.   What does Jesus say is his "sign"?
     But why is he indirect about it at this point?   How would his resurrection prove his authority?

C.   His new disciples' reactions, vv. 17-22

5.   As one of Jesus' new disciples, how would you feel? The author John, who is there as one of them, comments that Jesus' acts, his attitude and words make profound impressions on them. What do they learn about their new Master?

D.   The crowd's belief, vv. 23-25

6.   As a result of the temple clean-up and other "signs" of Jesus' authority, how do many in the Passover crowd respond to Jesus?   (vv. 23-25)
7.   What do you think they see in Jesus that attracts them? Why does Jesus "not trust himself to them"?   What kind of followers does a leader want?

Practical Themes — Choose the appropriate one.

a)   Compare some modern revolutionary leader with Jesus. What is similar?   What is different?   What makes Jesus a believable leader whom men can trust?   What kind of leader do you instinctively trust?
b)   Of the three groups who variously responded to Jesus' authority that day at the temple, which can you identify with — the Jewish leaders?   the disciples? the crowd?   In what ways?

2 He Crashes the Traditional Barriers
John 4:1-30

Introduction: Why do many white people refuse to live in a neighbourhood where there are non-white residents? Why does a mother object if her daughter wants to marry a man from a lower social class? Why do we feel superior to those from a certain province or dialect? The word "prejudice" literally means "to judge before" (one has examined the truth).

Notes on the Text

v. 1   *John* See Word List.

v. 4f   *Samaria* See Word List.

v. 5   *Jacob, Joseph* Ancestors of both Jews and Samaritans. Cf. vv. 6, 12.

v. 6   *sixth hour* Noon by Jewish reckoning.

v. 20   *this mountain . . . Jerusalem* A long-standing controversy.

v. 21   *Father* A radical concept of God to her.

v. 25   *the Messiah* See Word List.

Study/Discussion Questions

A. Facing the barriers, vv. 1-8 (9, 20, 27)

1. Read through the whole passage to see what prejudices Jesus overcomes in this personal conversation with the woman. What are they? Also, what do you observe about his own physical condition?
    What is Jesus risking in spending time in public with an adulterous woman of a despised race?

2. Note Jesus' seemingly insignificant opening. What does it reveal of his understanding about human nature?

B. Engaging the person, vv. 9-20

3. What seems to be the woman's first reaction to Jesus? Then how do you see Jesus, step by step, causing her attitude to change?
4. The main topic in the first half of the conversation is "living water". What amazing things does he say about this living water? Why do you think she does not understand his meaning?
5. At this point Jesus suddenly tells her to call her husband. Why?
   Observe how the woman tries to change the subject. What does she talk about? How does Jesus handle this religious distraction?

C. Revealing his identity, vv. 21-30

6. How would you describe the woman thus far? What is remarkable about her? What do you think Jesus sees in her and her situation?
   What is his ultimate aim in the conversation? In what way does he achieve this aim?
7. What two things in vv. 28-29 show that the woman is evidently convinced that Jesus is the Messiah?
   What do you think are the different things about the conversation and about Jesus himself that convince her he is completely trustworthy?

Practical Themes — Choose the appropriate one.

a) What strikes you most in this conversation? What can you learn from this?
b) What values and prejudices motivate you in your relationship with others? Can you identify with Jesus in his values? Or with the woman in her search for permanent spiritual reality and satisfaction?

3 He Challenges the Holiness Concept
John 5:1-18

Introduction: People have different ideas about what is holy. But usually there are common ideas of a place (temple, mosque, church), or an activity (praying, burning joss sticks, fasting during Ramadan) or an object used in worship (beads, wheels, altar). In Jesus' day, people who should have known better had wrong ideas about what is holy. Their artificial concept clashed with Jesus' view.

Notes on the Text

v. 1   *feast*   An unnamed Jewish holy celebration, the reason for Jesus' being in Jerusalem again.

v. 2   *five porticoes* Five spacious porches around the pool.

vv. 3b-4 These verses, not found in the most dependable ancient manuscripts, were probably added later to explain why people came there. It is not suggested that the waters were healing, only that people thought so.

v. 8   *pallet* Mat or mattress.

v. 9   *sabbath* See Word List.

v. 10   *the Jews* See Word List.

Study/Discussion Questions

A.   Do you want to be healed? vv. 1-9

1.   Observe the man whom Jesus chooses to help. From what is implied in vv. 3-7, how would you describe his condition? Why has his faith so far been inadequate to bring results? Reflect on v. 14 also.

2.   Examine v. 6. What is the key word in Jesus' simple question? By this question, what does Jesus want the man to realise for himself?

3. Note the three-part command he gives to the man. At which point do you think he is healed?

B. Who healed you? vv. 10-14

4. What is it that most impresses the Jews about the healing of a man who has been physically helpless for 38 years?!? Why do they not naturally marvel and rejoice? What does this reveal about their scale of values?

C. Why did Jesus heal on the sabbath? vv. 15-18

5. Consider Jesus' sole defense when his accusers face him with breaking (their interpretation of) the sabbath law. What is his concept of "work" according not only to v. 17, but the whole story?

6. How does Jesus' use of the sabbath day differ from the Jews? How then would he define his concept of what is truly holy and good?

7. Now we come to the issue more basic than the sabbath itself. As the leaders readily see, in what way does Jesus claim equality with God?
What does the Jews' refusal to believe Jesus in the face of evidence indicate about their concept of God? How does Jesus' concept of God differ?

Practical Themes — Choose the appropriate one.

a) Can you think of ways that show we consider things or activities or our viewpoints more important than people? If Jesus visited our religious institutions today what do you think he would attack as unbelief or God-distractions?

b) Note the sick man's weak will (vv. 5-7), his amazing ignorance of Jesus (vv. 11-12) and his lack of wisdom (vv. 15-16)! If Jesus healed such an unworthy man, would he help you with your past failures and present weaknesses?

4 He Gets Under the Surface (Parts 1, 2, 3)
Matthew 23:1-39

Introduction: This is Jesus' last public teaching, in the last week of his life, addressed to the crowds in Jerusalem as well as to his disciples. He knows his enemies are set to destroy him, for he contradicts their interpretation and application of Scripture. He threatens their social status and authority. Yet he continues to teach, challenging whatever is wrong in the religion of his people.

Part 1) Radical Humility, Mt. 23:1-12

Notes on the Text

v. 2   *scribes and Pharisees* See Word List.
         Moses' seat The spiritual/legal authority derived from Moses, the one through whom God gave his laws to Israel.

v. 5   *phylacteries* The leather arm- or head-band on which Scripture was written, worn probably only by the pious Pharisees.

v. 6   *synagogues* See Word List.

v. 8   *rabbi* See Word List.

v. 10   *master* Denotes personal authority in a certain area, clearly recognised by others.
          the Christ See "Messiah" in Word List.

122

Study/Discussion Questions

A. The leaders' love for recognition, vv. 1-7

1. Despite the generally heavy judgment Jesus makes on the scribes and Pharisees, what credit does he give them? What does he observe a) about their words and works? b) about their expectations of other people? c) about their intentions?

2. How does Jesus' evaluation of these leaders reveal his own values?

B. Jesus' standard for his disciples, vv. 8-11

3. Which one of the leaders' sins does Jesus warn his disciples about? What are his reasons that men ought not to love social recognition?
What social positions and titles do people strive after? Can we do without social recognition?

4. Is Jesus' concept of equality the same as our modern ideas on equality and brotherhood (which originate from the time of the French Revolution)?

5. Some people think that Jesus is preaching a kind of Christian anarchy here. Do you agree? Then how do you relate Jesus' concept of servanthood in v. 11 with the anarchist view of man?

6. According to Jesus, can a servant ever be a leader?

C. A radical conclusion, v. 12

7. Look at v. 12 carefully. These words are well-known and perhaps rather worn. How are these words abused? If Jesus is not preaching masochism, how do you explain his words here and in v. 11?

8. Compare these words with John 12:24. Jesus is not a theorist, for how do his life and his disciples' lives illustrate his words?
What should these words mean for us practically?

Part 2) The Inward and the Outward, Mt. 23:13-28

Notes on the Text

v. 15   *proselyte* In the NT, a Gentile convert to the Jewish faith.

v. 16f *temple, gold, altar, gift* Jesus is pointing out the Jews' lack of real discernment about which objects have ultimate spiritual value.

v. 23   *mint, dill and cummin* The most common garden herbs and tiny aromatic seeds.

v. 25   *cup and plate* Reference to the Jews' fastidious rituals for the purification of food containers.

Study/Discussion Questions

A.   The man behind the judgement, vv. 13-28

1.   Suppose this is the first time you are reading Jesus' words here. What are your impressions? Which words and ideas does he repeat?

2.   What kind of a man do you see behind these scathing words? Why is Jesus not afraid to make such direct judgments on the leaders?

B.   Barriers: words and deeds, vv. 13-15

3.   In v. 13 Jesus talks about stumbling-blocks which get in the way of the sinner who wants to repent. What are these stumbling-blocks?
Jesus goes on to say in v. 14 that the very behaviour of the Pharisees, though unknown to them, was a stumbling-block. What is the secret of knowing oneself?

4.   Compare v. 14 with Mt. 7:17-20. When God judges us, what counts ultimately in his eyes?
Why does Jesus use such strong language in calling a Pharisees' proselyte "a child of hell"?

5.   Are you aware of any barriers set up by Christians which might be preventing you from joining God's

people or entering his kingdom?   (i.e., outward things
– v. 13)
Are you aware of anything in your own life which might
hinder you from drawing nearer to God?   (i.e., inward
things – v. 14)

C.   Expediency and the law, vv. 16-24

In vv. 16-22, Jesus accuses the Pharisees of twisting the
law concerning oaths so that it would serve their own
ends. But they forget the essential aim of the law. How
human and up to date!
6.   The "weightier matters" of the law are justice, mercy
and faith. In this context, how does Jesus apparently
relate them to each other?

D.   Inward and outward realities, vv. 25-28

7.   If Jesus lived in our 20th century society, what comparisons might he use to describe the inner and the
outer characteristics of man?

Practical Themes – Choose the appropriate one.

a)   Jesus was always interested in the heart of man, in his
intents and motives (e.g., Mt. 15:11, 18). You may have
noticed in previous studies that he usually got "under
the surface" quickly in his encounters with people. Are
the thoughts and feelings in your private life always con-
sistent with your words and deeds?
b)   Is there any part of Jesus' description of the scribes and
Pharisees that seems to fit you?

Part 3) Past, Present & Future, Mt. 23:29-39

Notes on the Text

v. 30   *blood of the prophets* The OT records many instances of the Jews, killing God's prophets.

v. 31   *sons* This term often means "characteristic of", "having the nature of", without reference to physical relationship.

v. 34   Acts illustrates Jesus' prediction, e.g., Stephen, James, Paul.

v. 35   *Abel to Zechariah* See Gn. 4:8 and 2 Chronicles 24:21.

v. 38   *house* The temple, which was sacrilegously plundered and destroyed in AD 70 by the Romans.

Study/Discussion Questions

A.   Links with the past, vv. 29-33

1.   What does Jesus say are the Pharisees' reasons for honouring their ancient prophets? How does v. 31 indicate his reason for not believing they are sincere?
Can you suggest a contemporary example of a "pharisaical attitude" towards prophets and critics of society?

2.   According to Jesus' sharp words in vv. 32-33, why does he consider repentance not possible for the Pharisees (and any other people who remain deaf to God's promptings)?

B.   Lessons for the present, vv. 34-36

3.   Study the words "therefore" in v. 34 and "that" in v. 35. What reasons does your insight suggest for Jesus' sending wise men and prophets and teachers to us?
What principles from these radical words of Jesus apply to our own situation?

4.   In an age when individualism is strong, v. 36 is perhaps not easy to understand. Yet the previous verses hold the

clue to the meaning of this prophecy. How then, in the light of this context, would you interpret this verse? What is its relevance for us today?

C. Judgment in the future, vv. 37-39

5. Why does Jesus "suddenly" address Jerusalem? What emotions does the city arouse in him?
(Matthew wrote his gospel mainly for the Jewish community. Jesus' words must have shocked the Jews. Try to understand them from their viewpoint)
6. In what different ways can you recognise Jesus as the Radical yet Compassionate One here?

Review

7. After studying the whole chapter, how fair do you think Jesus' judgment on the Pharisees is?
8. Many people think of religion as an easy means of escape, an opiate. What is your opinion of the Christian faith after listening to Jesus' words in this chapter?
9. We may admire Jesus for his boldness, but inevitably the question arises. How does he look at our own times, and more specifically, how does he look at me? Can we escape a real encounter with him?

5 Who Shall Inherit the Earth?
Matthew 5:1-13

Introduction: Jesus has just begun his ministry as an itinerant rabbi. Like John the Baptist's, his basic message is, "Repent, for the kingdom of heaven is at hand" (Mt. 4:17). Many who have been prepared through John's baptism now look to Jesus, for he seems to be the Messiah John has said is coming. They have been long waiting for a political leader who could lead them in a revolution against their Roman oppressors. Would Jesus be this strong man? Would his teaching be the kind they want to hear and follow?

Notes on the Text

v. 3   *Blessed* An exclamation, "O the happiness of".
         kingdom of heaven See Word List.
v. 6   *righteousness* Cf. vv. 10, 21. See Word List.
v. 12   *prophets* See Word List.

Study/Discussion Questions

A.   What is happiness? vv. 1-12

1.   We must first try to imagine how a Jew would understand the word "blessed". What kind of person would they think is truly blessed? (Cf. Mark 10:23-26)
      How would you define happiness (blessedness)? In your opinion, who is blessed or happy?

2. Observe the contrasts Jesus uses here as a teaching method. Taking each verse in turn, discuss the following:
   — What is the present condition of the people Jesus describes as blessed? How do you usually think of and relate to such people? What do you usually expect to become of them in the future?
   — What is the relationship between the first and second half of each verse? How does it help you to define happiness?

B. How do we find happiness? vv. 3-10

3. Some of the verses seem contrary to common sense and contradict the "reasonable" standards we have adopted. Jesus wants to turn our thinking upside down!
   In your own words, what radical truth is Jesus communicating in these beatitudes?
   Think of one or two practical areas in your life where this truth is practically relevant.

C. Who are the salt of the earth? v. 13

4. Some people argue that Jesus is a fatalist who recommends in vv. 3-12 that we escape from this world and seek an "other worldly" kind of comfort. They say that he offers nothing but an opiate.
   What is your response to this argument? Is it a fair judgment? Think through your reasons carefully.

5. Observe how Jesus apparently foresees this reaction. How does he counter this argument in v. 13?

Reflection: What is the function of salt in food, particularly meat? In what way can people who are characterised by Jesus' beatitudes be called the "salt" of this earth? What practical things do you think Jesus had in mind? Which practical things might he have in mind for us, and for you personally?

A Final Word

The True Servant

Have this mind among yourselves, which you have in Christ Jesus, who, though he was in the form of God, did not count equality with God a thing to be grasped, but emptied himself, taking the form of a servant, being born in the likeness of men. And being found in human form he humbled himself and became obedient unto death, even death on a cross. Therefore God has highly exalted him and bestowed on him the name which is above every name, that at the name of Jesus every knee should bow, in heaven and on earth and under the earth, and every tongue confess that Jesus Christ is Lord, to the glory of God the Father. *Phil. 2:5-11*

1. As you reflect on Jesus' becoming a man, what seems to you his outstanding attitude? Have you ever thought of what our world would be like if he had not come to us like that?
2. What was his greatest act of obedience to God? Why was he willing to do this? What are the results of Jesus' obedience to God? their implications for all men?
3. At the opening we are asked, as human beings, to have the same mind as Jesus Christ, who was God. How do you think this applies to our human minds?
4. How do you envisage the fulfilment of this passage that "every knee shall bow . . . and every tongue confess that Jesus Christ is Lord"? How are we going to be his servants?

H The Call to Discipleship

The Christian faith is not meant to be an opiate or something merely to reflect upon. Living faith can move mountains. Living faith warms the heart of man. It opens his eyes and ears. It gives power to his feet and hands to follow the Master. It changes the direction of man's attention, of his goals and aims.

Jesus called a few fishermen to be his disciples. They were ordinary people, poor, uneducated and perhaps rather rough and insensitive. During the course of their discipleship they became what they were meant to be: instruments in the hands of God. When God uses an instrument, he uses it in the optimum way. He doesn't exploit or destroy it, but develops, teaches and helps it to realise its full potential.

But in the household of God, to human eyes, everything seems to have been turned upside-down. The meek and powerless will inherit the earth, the first will be the last, love is stronger than violence. And, as it is applied here, the ones who give themselves and forsake everything else, will receive the most and become true human beings. The cost of discipleship is one's very "life". The reward is a "new life".

1 Is He Master or Lord?
Luke 5:1-11

Introduction: From the first days of his public work Jesus became popular. He aroused great interest throughout the country. The common people were convinced that the words he spoke were full of power and authority. But Jesus knew that he could not minister personally to all. So he called out some men whom he could train more intensively to work with him.

Notes on the Text

v. 1   *Lake of Gennesaret* See "Galilee" in Word List.
v. 2   *fishermen* Cf. vv. 7, 10. He had called them before (Mk. 1:16-20).
v. 5   *all night* The usual time for fishing.
v. 8   *Depart from me* Simon Peter's acknowledgement that Jesus was a much greater person with greater powers than he had thought.
v. 11   *left everything* Including their substantial business (Mk. 1:20).

Study/Discussion Questions

A.   Some busy fisherman, vv. 1-7

1.   The clue in v. 5 indicates it is morning. What are possible reasons for the crowd's eager interest in Jesus? By contrast, what is different about Simon Peter and his friends' attitude?
2.   Note how Jesus moves from the crowd to the fishermen and then to one man. Why do you think that Jesus chooses Peter's boat to teach from?

3. Consider Peter's reaction each time Jesus asks him to do something. How do they differ? Why?
4. Watch the progressive steps by which the carpenter teacher caught the professional fishermen for his mission. What do these steps reveal about Jesus' understanding of their psychology?

B. An astonished sinner, vv. 7-10

5. What new things does Simon Peter see through the miracle? In which way do you think his exclamation is logical and expected? In which way is it not?
6. What are reasons that a man like Simon Peter would respond positively to a man like Jesus?

C. Fishers of men, vv. 10-11

7. At the beginning of his work Jesus called these men to follow him (Mk 1:16-20). They have observed him for about a year (Luke 4). But their association has not been a close, constant companionship. What qualities has Jesus apparently observed in them during that year that makes him choose them to be his co-workers?
8. What was the climactic response of Simon Peter and his partners to Jesus? What can make established businessmen leave "everything" to follow an itinerant teacher?

Practical Themes — Choose one for discussion.

a) From Peter's experience what can you learn about becoming Jesus' true disciple? What makes it easier for us than for him?
b) What can we learn from this passage about Jesus as a teacher and disciple maker? What would you like to imitate in him?
c) Have you ever considered leaving "everything" to follow Jesus Christ as your real Lord? What would "everything" mean for you?

2 Radical Discipleship
Luke 6:27-42

Introduction: The religious leaders saw the mounting popularity of Jesus. They challenged him, but he kept speaking the truth about God, even if it was against them. They determined to destroy him. Amidst this, Jesus chose twelve men among the many disciples to become his closest associates. Then he began to teach them and other sincere followers what serious discipleship in his kingdom means.

Notes on the Text

v. 27   *Love your enemies*   To "love your neighbour" (Lv. 19:18), the Pharisees had added "hate your enemies".

v. 30   *take away your goods*   The Roman soldiers occupying Palestine then could demand a limited amount of goods from the people.
       give   The tense is present continuous, i.e., "keep giving"!

v. 31   Others before expressed this "Golden Rule", but always negatively; i.e., "Don't do to others what you don't want them to do to you."

v. 38   *good measure*   Market measurements for grain and other goods.

vv. 41-42   *speck. . .log* Note Jesus' background in carpentry.

Study/Discussion Questions

A. The unusual audience

1. To whom does Jesus direct his message? (See vv.17, 20)
Imagine yourself in the audience. Which statements

catch your immediate attention? How do you react to them? Why? What does it make you think of Jesus?

B. The unusual teaching

2. What are the different kinds of person-to-person situations that Jesus discusses? How does Jesus teach his disciples to treat others in each case?
3. Remember the political situation then. Why do you think Jesus stresses loving one's enemies? Do you think Jesus intends his teaching to go beyond our national enemies? In what ways?
4. What makes people feel they have certain rights to criticise and condemn their neighbour? What positive attitudes and actions does Jesus substitute for judging others?

C. The unusual teacher

5. What does this passage tell us about Jesus as a teacher? about his methods? about his observation of human nature? about his main concerns?
    What hope for overcoming our human weaknesses does he give?
6. How could you summarise his message so that it rings with relevance today?

Practical Themes — Choose one for discussion.

a) Who are your enemies — people who raise feelings of hostility in you? What difference can Jesus make in these relationships?
b) Which of Jesus' instructions for his disciples do you find most difficult to carry out? Why?

3   In Whom We Trust
Luke 12:13-34

Introduction: After Cain had murdered his brother Abel, he restlessly wandered, seeking refuge. He settled in Nod ("wandering"). Finally he built a city to be safe behind its walls and live an independent life, free to follow his own desires (Gn. 4:8-17).

The city — symbol of human self-sufficiency! Babylon — symbol of man's endeavour to create human wisdom and find human identity apart from God! On what do we rely? On city walls, insurance companies, money, technology, human reasoning, rational planning?

Notes on the Text

v. 13   *inheritance and riches* A special interest in Luke's gospel.

v. 14   *Man* The only time Jesus uses this stern tone of address.

v. 20   *fool* Another strong word meaning "without sense".

v. 27   *Solomon* King David's son, symbol of wealth, beauty, wisdom.

. 31   *kingdom* See Word List.

v. 34   *heart* See Word List.

Study/Discussion Questions

A.   How not to save your life, vv. 13-21

1.   Our passage introduces us to one of Cain's spiritual descendents. Why does this man come out of the crowd to Jesus? What kind of answer to his request does he apparently expect?

2. Why does Jesus begin his answer with a question? Then how does his parable answer the man's real problem of covetousness?
3. Marx has said that capitalism is the source of greed, which is not a natural vice of man but imposed on him by society. According to Marx, man cannot help being greedy. What does Jesus say about greed and its source? How are we to overcome it in the light of this passage?

B. In whom we trust, vv. 22-31

In this section Jesus expands what he means by "being rich towards God".
4. Analyse v. 22 and 23 and also v. 15b. Try paraphrasing Jesus' teaching in these verses.
5. How do you measure the value of your life? By your possessions and material things? Or by what other measure?
6. What specific things about "being rich towards God" do Jesus' references to ravens, lilies and grass teach us? How does Jesus relate all this to seeking God's kingdom?
7. List all the characteristics of God you can find, citing the verses.

C. Fears and treasures, vv. 32-34

8. What fears about possessions and life does Jesus know his disciples have? His advice in v. 33 then is radical, but in what ways does he show that it is the wise course to take?
9. Discuss the effect which possessions have on a man's will and ambition, and even on his time, his emotions, his personal relationships, and finally his heart.
How are our heart, our treasures and our fears all related?

4 Count the Cost
Luke 14:25-35

Introduction: On this last journey to Jerusalem, many who followed Jesus were looking for a leader to bring them worldly power and liberation from political oppressors. But Jesus was introducing a spiritual kingdom and bringing inner freedom to men — freedom from self-seeking, freedom to sacrifice one's own life for him and for others. Jesus freely extended the invitation to his kingdom to all who humbly admitted their need. But he also squarely presented to the crowds the personal cost of following him.

Study/Discussion Questions

A. The cost of renouncing, vv. 25-27

1. In what kind of situation can love for people nearest us seem like hate?   What does Jesus want to express by the word "hate"?   So, what is Jesus actually asking from would-be followers?   Why do you think Jesus included "and even his own life"?   How can such a commitment be possible in our lives?
2. Jesus does not ask us for more than he gave. What did the cross mean for him?   What does "bearing our own cross" mean for us?
3. Think through the full implications of v. 27. Why do you think Jesus makes this hard statement that seems to destroy personal freedom and identity?   Compare vv. 26-27 with Galatians 5:13 and 1 Corinthians 9:19.

    For you were called to freedom, brethren; only do not use your freedom as an opportunity for the flesh, but through love be servants of one another. . . For though I am free from all men, I have made myself a slave to all, that I might win the more.

    What underlying principle do you see in these texts concerning the (true) human attitude to one's neighbour?

138

B. The cost of continuing, vv. 28-30

4. How humiliating for a builder to be unable to complete his work! What kind of "foundation" might a potential disciple of Christ lay? Why might his work remain unfinished? What is missing?

C. The cost of refusing his terms, vv. 31-33

5. Jesus' next illustration about the hostile kings has similarities with the one about the builder. But its dissimilarities reveal a slightly different point. What kind of decision does the 10,000-army king face? What does Jesus imply is the only sensible decision for him to make? Why?

6. Who do you think Jesus intends the kings to represent? What other kind of cost, then, does he want potential disciples to calculate?

7. In what way can "sit down first" and "take counsel" be applied to us? In what sense are we to renounce all we have?

D. Tasteless salt, vv. 34-35

8. What are the properties of salt? How can these illustrate what a Christian's lifestyle and influence in the world should be? How is cheap discipleship like tasteless salt?

Reflection: Do you have "ears to hear" these words of Jesus? It takes courage to count the cost of discipleship — courage to stop pretending, courage to take account of the costs realistically. Think through what the costs in your life are concretely and practically. Think through, too, what it will cost not to follow Jesus Christ on his terms.

Many people are willing to pay lip-service to Jesus Christ, yet are not prepared to walk the way of the cross. Others have made a quick decision to follow him and were perhaps aware of some immediate costs, but not of the much higher, future ones. Still others (perhaps all of us?) try to avoid paying those costs and look for an easier, "cheaper" life (What kind?), or pay with counterfeit currency (How?).

5 The Ultimate Test of Life
Matthew 7:13-29

Introduction: Here are the concluding words of Jesus' sermon on the mount. His preceding teaching might well be interpreted by some as a meditation on the higher values of life or the revelation of a special road to be trod by particularly religious, sensitive souls. But these final words of Jesus leave no room for this. It is an "either-or" situation. It is life or death. It is confessing and serving Jesus Christ — choosing the narrow, hard way — or taking it easy and missing the main road.

Notes on the Text

v. 13   *the way*   The guidelines in our life, the goal we choose, the significant steps we take.

v. 15   *false prophets*   People who seem to be God's spokesmen, but whose motives and intentions are false.

v. 22   *that day*   The day of the Lord, the day of judgment, when all hidden things in our lives will be brought out into the open.

v. 24   *these words of mine*   Jesus' teachings in Ch. 5:1 — 7:12.

Study/Discussion Questions

A.   Two gates, two roads, vv. 13-14

1.   First, discuss a preliminary and important question: What might the "gate" mean in our personal life? In the context of the whole sermon, what do you think Jesus means by the "narrow" and the "wide" gates?

2.   Here Jesus calls the way of his Gospel hard, and elsewhere he teaches it is simple, understood only by children. Why?

3. What kind of life does each road imply? Why does Jesus relate the nature of each road to its final destination (life or death)?
   How can we know which road we are on?

B. **Many false prophets, vv. 15-20**

4. How does Jesus teach us to detect false prophets? Is this merely a matter of subjective opinion, or is it based on objective fact?
5. What is the "wolf-likeness" of these false prophets? What kind of people does Jesus evidently have in mind? Do they have their equivalent in our age?

C. **Two foundations of life, vv. 21-29**

6. In v. 23, the judgment Jesus himself will pronounce on certain "Christian" doers sounds harsh. But on what basis does he say it will be based? How fair do you consider it?
7. In what ways does the passage in vv. 24-27 relate to the previous two sections on false prophets and professional "Christian" doers?
   Reflect on v. 24 — "these words of mine". "To the extent we put these words into practice we will understand them." Is there another way of understanding them? What produces consistency in a person?
8. To what does Jesus liken the rock? What is he saying about himself by this?

Practical Themes — Choose one for discussion.

a) In what way do you find the Gospel "narrow" and "hard"? Are the really good things in life usually easy and readily attainable?
b) Try to put in concrete and practical words what it would mean to "build your house on the rock".
c) What kind of fruits do you think you should be producing? How can you start?

A Final Word

The Two Circles

Everyone who believes that Jesus is the Christ is a child of God, and every one who loves the parent loves the child. By this we know that we love the children of God, when we love God and obey his commandments. For this is the love of God, that we keep his commandments. And his commandments are not burdensome. For whatever is born of God overcomes the world; and this is the victory that overcomes the world, our faith. Who is it that overcomes the world but he who believes that Jesus is the Son of God? *I John 5:1-5*

Faith in Jesus Christ is no mere invention of man. If it were, it would be no more than a projection of his own image onto a meaningless figure who lived 2000 years ago. In pretending to obey that person he would only be following his own desires. This is certainly a possibility: *this is the first circle.*

Faith is a gift from God, but it must be *received.* There is no such thing as a passive recipient here, for he must actively accept what is being offered: a dynamic power which can conquer the world, and conquer self, a power which will enable him to trust and love God. The love of God makes it possible for us to love one another; it is no noble idea, but rather in Jesus Christ it is reality. And for the one who believes, faith and reality become linked as he keeps God's commandments. *This is the second circle.*

The question on which the above Bible passage ends provides the clue as to how one can leave the first circle and enter the second. Read this verse twice and insert your own name.

Word List

Abraham The first Jew whom God called to begin a new race through which he could bless the rest of the world; lived about 2000-1800 B.C.

age to come Life in heaven, or the time when Jesus Christ will make all things new in his visible kingdom.

Capernaum A fishing town on the NW shore of the Sea of Galilee, important enough to have a tax collector and a Roman military post. Jesus made it the base of his ministry after his own people in Nazareth rejected him.

chief priests The most influential religious leaders, mainly Sadduccees, and members of the Sanhedrin, the nation's ruling council.

Decapolis The Gentile "Ten Towns", E and SE of the Sea of Galilee.

denarius, denarii (pl.) Roman coin representing a labourer's daily wage.

Devil Sometimes called Satan or the prince of this world. The one who obstructs and tries to destroy the work of God. Instead of obeying God as the Creator and Lord of the universe, man turned away and submitted himself to other powers of which the Devil is the head.

eternal life The indestructible and highest quality of life beginning here; the timeless vertical dimension of human life, continuing hereafter in the direct presence of the holy and personal God.

Galilee, Sea of Also referred to as the Sea of Tiberias or Lake of Genneseret in the northern region of Galilee (Jesus' home province), bordered by the towns of Capernaum, Bethsaida etc., a lake some 13 miles long and 7 miles broad, with fish plenteous enough for export. Winds sweeping down from the surrounding mountains on this crater lake often caused sudden, violent storms.

God Like the potter designing and making pottery, so God is the creator of man. How may finite man, though God has made him in his divine image, come to know the Infinite One who has created him, his world, time, his desires, his mind? By himself he cannot. But God reveals himself to man as a personal Spirit who loves and fulfils his plan in spite of man's efforts to hinder it. Man cannot prove the existence of God, but God speaks: "I am who I am", expressing his sovereignty; and he speaks again and again through his prophets and above all through his Son Jesus Christ.

heart Regarded in the Bible as the seat of the intellect, will and feelings; the core of man's personality.

Herod's party, Herodians A political faction whose pro-Romanism alienated them from other Jews, especially the anti-Roman Pharisees, but who also sought to destroy Jesus, because he challenged their morality and threatened their political security.

Jericho A city rich by balsam and olive groves and international trade, 15 miles from Jerusalem and 3,000 feet lower; a favourite resort of Herodian royalty as well as thousands of priests.

Jerusalem "City of peace", dating from the 2nd millenium BC; the beloved national capital of the Jews in the southern region of Judea; often used as a symbol of the whole Jewish nation; political/religious storm center of opposition to Jesus.

Jesus of Nazareth His earthly social identity. (See "Nazareth")

the Jews In John's Gospel this term refers to the Jerusalem religious leaders.

John the Baptist (Not to be confused with John, "the beloved disciple" who wrote the fourth Gospel) He prepared Israel for the coming of Jesus as the Messiah by his powerful, fearless preaching and baptising people who genuinely repented from their sins. He was Jesus' cousin, older by six months, but apparently did not know him personally, having lived as an ascetic in the Judean deserts.

Kingdom of God, (Heaven) The reign of God over the new community of people redeemed by Christ's salvation of grace. The Jews had for centuries looked forward to this Messianic kingdom, but in Jesus' day the concept had become largely political and materialistic. Matthew, writing to Jews, uses "kingdom of heaven", a Jewish custom of avoiding overfamiliarity with the name of God.

the Law Often referred to as "the law of Moses"; the first five books of the OT, containing the first major events of man's history, the early history of the Jewish nation and particularly their rules and regulations given by God through Moses. Sometimes the term is used in a general sense of the whole OT.

Lord (JAHWEH) Hebrew title stressing God's sovereign eternal nature.

Messiah Hebrew for "the Christ" (Gk), originally a title meaning "the anointed one", i.e., the one God chose and sent as universal, eternal Saviour and Lord of all men.

Moses One of the greatest OT heroes whom God used as liberator of his Jewish people from Egyptian slavery and as law-giver during their wilderness travels between Egypt and the promised land of Canaan; lived about 1400 BC.

name For the Jews the name of a person was more than just a label or number. A man's very identity was expressed by his name, and in the Kingdom of God, when man's real identity will be revealed, every man will receive a new name.

Nazareth A small market town belonging to the tribe of Zebulun in southern Galilee. It had a bad reputation partly because of its history (Is. 9:1a), and partly because of low moral standards that overnight caravan traders encouraged. But see Is. 9:1b.

outer darkness Separation from God, who is eternal light; hell.

parable A brief but vivid story picture of something concrete and familiar, used to illustrate a lasting truth.

Passover feast A major Jewish feast in early spring observing God's miraculous deliverance of the Jews' ancestors from

Egyptian slavery. The angel of death killed the first-born in Egyptian homes, but "passed over" the Hebrew homes which had lambs' blood smeared over their doors. This foreshadowed the later sacrificial death of Jesus to save people from judgment. See Ex. 12:18-27, Dt. 16:5-8.

Pharisees "The separated ones". A rather exclusive Jewish religious party which prided itself in strict observance of the Law of Moses and the hundreds of traditional interpretations added to it through the centuries. Middle-class and anti-Roman, they thus were political/religious opponents of the Sadduccees, who were aristocratic, pro-Roman and less popular.

prophet A spokesman for God not only to predict what important events will come but to apply His Word practically to contemporary society.

rabbi Also "Rabboni", derived from the Hebrew word meaning "great". It came to mean "my teacher" or "my master". A highly respectable title acknowledging a man's ability to teach the OT law rather than an academic status.

righteous, righteousness The quality of rightness, fairness; acceptance or vindication before God.

ruler An elder who arranged synagogue services, kept its proprieties and looked after other community affairs. Some were members of the national supreme council (Sanhedrin).

sabbath The seventh day of the Jewish week, on which God intended His people to rest from ordinary work and celebrate His goodness. This, of all the OT commandments, became the most weighted down with traditional interpretations, burdening and confusing the people. Thus its observance became the symbol of the bitter controversy between the Pharisees and Jesus.

Sadduccees A small religious party, composed mainly of priestly aristocrats, very influential with the wealthy. They accepted only the first five books of the OT as authoritative. Therefore, unlike the opposing Pharisaic party, they rejected anything supernatural like angels, immortality, resurrection. To them the material world was the only reality. Politically they were liberal, compromising with the Romans with whom they felt their positions secure. Their number dominated the Sanhedrin.

Samaria The pure-blooded Jews despised the Samaritans, whose Jewish ancestors had inter-married foreigners about 700 years before, thus deviating culturally and religiously. Samaria lay between Judea and Galilee, and orthodox Jews took a longer detour across the Jordan River to avoid contamination.

Sanhedrin The highest Jewish tribunal in Jerusalem, traditionally originating with the 70 elders who assisted Moses (Nu. 11:16-24). They exercised varying degrees of power even under foreign rulers. During the time of Christ the Romans allowed it extensive jurisdiction, e.g., capital punishment with Roman confirmation.

scribes Teachers or lawyers who studied and taught the Jewish law. Their custom of dividing the 613 commandments of the law into "weighty" and "light" laws caused much academic debate on which were more important.

Simon Peter He was the most prominent of Jesus' twelve closest disciples, a fisherman like his brother Andrew, who introduced him to Jesus. He was from Jesus' own Galilean province. Though impetuous at times, he became a faithful leader and evangelist missionary in the first-century church.

Son of David A title for the Messiah, whom the Jews expected to descend from and succeed their glorious King David.

Son of Man Jesus often referred to himself as the Son of Man, a title for the Messiah derived from Dn. 7:13. Here the Son of Man is the one who will finally have dominion over mankind. Also, it is clear from the way Jesus used this title that he linked it with his suffering and death. He, the Son of God, identified with man, became one of the people, died for them, saved them and, as their servant, will be their future leader and shepherd.

synagogue Local meeting place for Jews to worship, learn the law and carry on community activities.

Tabernacles, Feast of A major Jewish feast, celebrating God's guidance and provision for the ancient Hebrews when they lived in tents (tabernacles) during their wilderness journeys. It lasted eight days in early October.

talent Worth about 6000 Roman denarii. One talent would be roughly the amount of money the average worker would earn during his lifetime.

tax collectors Hated by their fellow Jews because they worked for the colonial Romans and because they were outrageously dishonest.

teachers of the law See "scribes".

temple The national center for worship of God for the Jews, especially for the great feast days when animal sacrifices were made by the priests. The one standing in Jesus' day was built by Herod the Great, begun in 9 BC, finished in AD 64 and destroyed in AD 70 by the Romans.

woman Jesus used this address five times, a more personal term than the English suggests.